Photos

Introduction

The 1940s and 50s were unique times to be a boy, especially one living in the country, where a close neighbor was a quarter or a half mile away and the woods started at your back door. I grew up in such a setting in Blackberry, a rural township in north central Minnesota, near Grand Rapids. Those were the years just after the Great Depression and World War II. It was a time when people struggled with physical labor (some farmers still used workhorses), and there were wilderness places I could explore without people trespassing on my solitude.

Those who lived in Blackberry might read this account and say, "It wasn't like that at all." They are probably right. The names of many individuals have been changed, except in a few cases where the subject has long since been dead, or the stories do not reflect poorly on the individual. And this is not meant to be an absolute account of facts. It is, however, the truth—the truth as perceived through the eyes of a boy, overhearing only parts of conversations, catching snippets of gossip, and seeing the world through a child's eyes.

Chapter One

Mom was tiny, five feet tall and barely 100 pounds, but in my memory, she walks down a dusty country road carrying nine months of extra weight. She wears a navy blue maternity smock, one of the few she has to her name. Its underarms and bodice are soaked with perspiration that flows freely in the ninety degree heat of the August day. She is exhausted and can hardly stand on her swollen feet.

During that summer, the summer of 1953, she became increasingly heavy with pregnancy. Still, she had continued to work, sweating in the kitchen over a steaming pressure cooker, picking berries and garden produce to put up for the coming winter, washing clothes, and cooking meals. There was no rest, no summer vacation for my mother; the food she canned would have to last us through the winter.

I was ten years old, dressed in a ratty T-shirt and tattered hand-me-down pants, and I was happy with my life. That country road was my sandbox, my contact with the outside world, my bicycle racetrack, and my pathway to dreams fulfilled. It was my counselor's office that day with Mom. As we walked along, Mom worked, as she so often did, on magnetizing my moral compass to point in the right direction.

"Dennis, sometimes I get so afraid," she told me, her brow furrowed with care. "You'll have to leave here someday, you know."

"I know, Mom. I'll be okay." I felt lazy in the heat.

"But you don't know," Mom insisted. "If you end up in a city, there are so many bad things. There's something called heroin. People put it in their arms with needles, and it takes over their minds. Then they can't live without it. Don't ever take anything like that if someone gives it to you."

"I won't, Mom," I sighed. "I promise."

We didn't walk far. It was about time for Dad to return from work in the Danube Pit, a mine on the western end of the Mesabi Iron Range, and he expected Mom to have supper ready for the family. Mom turned heavily on her heels, and we headed back home.

That evening, after the dishes were done, a breeze picked up. When the phone rang, I imagined the conversation from the other end.

"How're you doing, Gen?" Mom's friend Mae would be saying. "It was so hot today." Mae was of Finnish descent, and she spoke with a gentle accent.

"You know how it is," I heard Mom answer. "I'm sure the baby dropped yesterday. At least I feel different today. More heavy or something." It was quiet as Mom listened to Mae, and I strained to hear. "Oh Mae, I can't tell you how I'd appreciate that," said Mom gratefully after a moment. "I really am bushed tonight. I scrubbed all the floors today. I don't know what got into me."

At eight-thirty I found out what Mom was excited about; Mae pulled up to take my sister Janice and I to a movie at the baseball field. "Jump in, kids," she said, and we were so excited we could hardly sit still. We were going to a real drive-in movie.

Mae drove us one mile to Highway 2 in her 1948 Chevrolet that was no better at smoothing out the washboard road than Dad's Ford. We crossed the little used highway and stopped at Blackberry's baseball field. Its outfield fence was a dense stand of red pines, and the outfield itself was full of divots and rocks. Up behind home plate, the backstop was made of hole-riddled chicken-wire fencing strung between old timbers.

This was our drive-in theater. Against the backstop, a screen made of white bed-sheets was hoisted like a sail, and a 1930s panel truck was backed onto the pitcher's mound. Its front end faced to the outfield, while the rear doors opened to expose the movie projector inside.

About twenty viewers were on hand for the big event. A couple of families waited inside their cars to escape the mosquitoes that swarmed out of the woods in the evening. I searched behind the backstop for baseballs that had been hit foul and never found while, nearby, a group of teenagers were jostling each other and talking loudly.

As dusk became almost night, the film started. I and a few others lay on the infield grass, and the adults sat on blankets. I caught my breath when the words "*The Green Arrow*" flickered onto the screen. It was a serial, and the narrator recapped:

"Last week, we left our hero hanging from a thin rope suspended between two buildings. He was crossing hand over hand, high above the street, but was discovered by his arch enemies who now have him trapped."

Brief flashes of last week's episode played for about two minutes. Then Green Arrow, a common, everyday person in disguise, shot one of his green-fletched arrows into another building. Attached to the arrow was a thin cord. Green Arrow took a detour on that line and escaped his enemies to fight another day.

The serial ended with two minutes of a teaser to get us to come back the next week.

I glanced behind me when I heard a car rattle to a stop in the parking lot. Dad got out in a hurry and talked to Mae for a couple of minutes. By then, Hop Along Cassidy was doing his thing on the screen, and I was so lost in a world of men wearing white or black hats that I hardly noticed when Mom and Dad drove off again.

When the movie ended, we tiredly piled into the car. Mae turned to my sister and I. "You kids are going to sleep at my house tonight," she said, smiling. "Your mom and dad are heading to the hospital, and by tomorrow, you'll have a baby brother or sister."

Then, like a scripted movie, the sky was split by a streak of lightening and rain started to fall, washing the August heat from the air. Janice and I rode through the deluge to a strange house and a strange bed. Mae tucked us in.

It seemed like I only closed my eyes for a second. When I opened them, it was light outside, and the rain had stopped. I crept downstairs in last night's clothes to find Mae in the kitchen preparing breakfast. When she saw me peek around the door frame, she grinned.

"Good morning," she said, still smiling. "You have a baby brother."

Chapter Two

Genevieve Burns, my mother, grew up in the small Iron Range town of Keewatin and spent her childhood as a town girl. She was accustomed to having neighbors, walking to the local grocery store, and playing on the schoolyard swings. Her house had an indoor toilet and a sink with hot and cold running water. The washing machine sat out in the enclosed back porch, and a hose could be run from the faucet to fill it.

In 1941, when Gen graduated from high school, the Great Depression still gripped the entire country by the throat, and my grandfather had the impossible task of providing for his eight sons and two daughters. Mom's oldest brother Percy was her favorite. He was more refined, and he treated her well. Percy became the fire chief in Keewatin and was respected in the community. Even after she married Dad, Percy was the one member of her family that encouraged her and made her feel important.

In Iron Range communities, almost every family was dubbed with a nickname. Some weren't very kind. The nickname for the members of the Burns family was "Monkey." Mom hated that name as much as her looks, though I always thought she was pretty. She had thick light brown hair that had a natural wave above her forehead. She was petite with a well proportioned figure. Mom, however, never saw herself that way.

Mom's grades in school were above average, and she had particularly enjoyed French. She would sing French ditties to me and Janice as she worked around home and even tried to teach me a few French words. Intelligent as she was, my mother's life goals were not lofty. After high school, as she told me later, she wanted to learn the beautician trade.

"Pa, all I need is a little help," she pleaded as her father read the paper. "Tuition isn't much. I can pay you back in installments."

"No." My grandfather's teeth clamped down on his pipe. "You'll just end up married, and then the money will be wasted."

Tears ran down Mom's face. "Please Pa, it's not much."

Mom's father ignored her tears and continued to read his paper. "Percy's brother-in-law, Louis, owns a grocery store over by Grand Rapids in Blackberry Township," he told her. "He needs a clerk in the store and someone to help clean for him and his wife. I've already told him you'd take the job."

The next week, when the ticket-master at the bus station gave his call ("Nashwauk, Pengilly, Calumet, Marble, Bovey, Coleraine, and Grand Rapids"), the eighteen-year-old who would become my mother boarded the bus. She didn't realize she was leaving home for good. She switched buses in Grand Rapids, taking the one headed east, to Duluth. Seven miles from Grand Rapids she reached up, pulled the cord that signaled it was her stop, and set foot for the first time in Blackberry.

Blackberry was a century from Keewatin. The store where Mom worked had cold running water, at least, but the outhouse behind was a new experience for her. The only other business establishment was another bit of a store a quarter mile down the highway. That was Blackberry. The population was dispersed over the many square miles of the township.

Almost all the young men from the area were in CCC camps or preparing to fight in the war. Only old men and the few others who couldn't pass the physicals were left home. For an eighteen-year-old girl, the experience in Blackberry was like being stuck in purgatory.

Her days were spent taking down canned goods from the shelves behind the counter after customers pointed out what they wanted. She had to restock the shelves, candle the fresh eggs brought in by local farmers (holding them up to a bright lightbulb to make sure there were no developing chicks inside), scrub the meat case, sweep the floor, and even clean the living quarters in the back of the store. The store was only the size of a living room. It was busy most of the time, but the evenings and nights were unbearably lonely.

Mom had three brothers in the military. Two were in the Marine Corps, and her sixteen-year-old brother Billy was on a destroyer somewhere near Hawaii. She had no one in Blackberry with whom she could share her sorrow, her loneliness, and her worry for her family. She would dream alone.

I wonder what Tony is doing now? I was a fool not to accept his proposal—why didn't I? God, I wish there was someone to talk to.

And between bouts of loneliness, she would wonder, *How am I ever going to meet anyone else to marry here? I'll probably end up with someone like old Emil, the hermit.*

As she walked down the dusty country road that ran south past the store, she dreamed of being swept off her feet and taken out of her miserable, lonely life. Thus, when a young man with a Zeus-like physique walked into the store, she nearly jumped into his arms.

He was six feet tall, two hundred pounds of muscle and bone, and he joked about things, laughed easily. To Mom, trapped in the middle of nowhere, he was a knight in shining armor. Edward Herschbach was one of the few single young men left in the area. He had tried to enlist in every branch of service but had failed all the physicals. He was a logger and a miner who looked anything but

4F, unfit for service, but every time he took a physical, the examiners sent him home without telling him what was wrong. They just said they couldn't use him.

He was seven years older than Mom, and so, when after a very short courtship they married on January 30, 1942, he was twenty-six and she was only nineteen. But she was out of the store. She had someone to care for her.

Chapter Three

When Mom and Dad were first married, Dad worked in the woods, supervising a crew of loggers for a company that made wooden bullet boxes. The job didn't pay well, and Mom and Dad moved into a tiny resort cabin. The rent was cheap, not only because it was the middle of winter in northern Minnesota, but also because the cabin was only about twelve by sixteen feet. That was Mom's honeymoon home.

Why did I ever listen to Pa? she must have wondered. *I should have just gone to Hibbing and tried to live alone. And I wonder what happened to Tony? Someone said he found a job. If I had married* him, *I'd at least be in a house with a toilet. How am I ever going to survive this winter, let alone this kind of life?*

She survived.

In the spring, the rent went up for the tourist season. The tiny cabin became too expensive for my parents, and they moved in with my grandmother, Dad's mother, and her unmarried daughter.

Grandma had been widowed at an early age, and she and my aunt lived on a small farm.

My aunt worked as hard as any man, mucking out the cow stalls, pitching hay, and digging in the garden. She had muscles suited for the jobs. Grandma, however, looked as though she had already spent the last of her physical reserve. She was skinny as a rail, and she always wore her gray hair in a braid wound around her head. Every dress she owned looked the same, some kind of faded flower print with hems down to her ankles and belted waists under her absolutely flat chest.

My family's roots, on Dad's side, were pure German. His people had moved north from New Ulm, Minnesota, and brought with them many characteristic traits associated with their heritage. Perhaps it wasn't that they were German; perhaps they were just the way they were. Nevertheless, they placed a disproportionate value on thriftiness and hard work.

After Grandpa Joe died, Dad continued to live at home and work the family farm. The farm was average size for Blackberry, about one-hundred-sixty acres. They raised a few chickens, a half dozen cows, and a pig or two. Almost all the work was done by hand or with a team of horses. The barn and most of the outbuildings were made of logs, and the house, although substantially built of rough-sawed lumber, was sealed from the weather with black tarpaper.

"Gen, it's five o'clock," Mom heard the first morning at my grandmother's. "Time to get up and start the day."

Mom struggled out of bed.

"We don't sleep all day around here," my grandmother continued. "After you do the breakfast dishes, go out and weed the garden."

Grandma laid out Mom's whole day. In the meantime, my aunt was already working on farm chores. "Gen better pull her own weight around here," she grumbled.

Some of Dad's sisters, especially those who lived close by, thought of Mom as an indentured servant.

"Gen, the stove needs more wood. Split a few armloads. The axe is stuck in the chopping block." And then when Mom tried to lift the heavy axe: "Get out of the way. With your puny swings, it'll take all day."

"Gen, the chimneys to the kerosene lamps need cleaning. Don't streak them this time."

"Get the hoe from the shed. Do you think you can hoe the rutabagas without messing up?"

When Dad came home from work, Grandma spoke only German to him so Mom could never understand what she was saying. Dad answered in English but didn't tell his mother to speak English when Mom was around. Mom got little support from him.

The incident with the work pants was the last straw. Mom had patched and re-patched this particular pair so many times that there was literally nothing left of the original material. Finally, Mom dumped them in the trash. Grandma found the pants, took them out of the trash, then sat down and sewed more patches on the patches. "Look at what your lazy wife was going to throw out," Grandma said when Dad came home from work. "I dug them out of the trash and mended them for you."

Not long after, Mom and Dad moved into a rented, dilapidated house. Evidently they must have had some privacy during that summer, because, if my math is correct, I was conceived sometime in July or August of 1942.

Chapter Four

When I was older, Mom told me about her stay in the hospital when she gave birth to me. Dad came into Mom's room after she had delivered.

"I want you to know that if anything happens to my son, I am holding you personally responsible, no matter what," he told her, his voice showing no tenderness. Then he left the room.

Mom was twenty years old at the time.

Later, the nurse came in carrying a bed pan.

"Now, Mrs. Herschbach, we don't want you to get out of bed, so use this bedpan," the nurse said. "You've been through a lot. It will take time to build your blood up."

During the days of forced bed rest, Mom held me and nursed me, learning as she went. On the fifth day, the nurse came into her room in the morning. "Good Morning, Mrs. Herschbach," she said with a smile. "It's time we got you out of bed."

Mom sat up and swung her feet over the edge of the bed. As the blood rushed to her toes, she became lightheaded and the color left her face. Her nurse helped her off the bed, and on rubber-band legs, she slowly walked down the hall and back.

Two days later she was able to go home, weak as a limp noodle. From the very beginning, she nurtured me in ways that I can still feel. One day when I was an adult, I told Mom I remembered things that happened when I was less than two years old. I could tell by her face that she didn't believe me. "That's impossible," she said. "You only think you remember, because you've heard me tell about those years."

"You used to hold me in your lap with a blanket wrapped around me," I insisted. "I remember the house was always cold in the winter, and the only heat was a fancy wood stove that sat in the middle of the living room."

"That's true, I did. You were sick so much that winter." She gave me a startled look. "What *else* do you remember?"

I had been born in early April of 1943, and my parents were renting a house that was covered with tarpaper. It was high quality tarpaper, though, with a faux brick pattern that was made of tiny brown granules of rock pressed into warm tar. The roof was sealed with paper that had green-dyed granules pressed onto its surface. In essence, we lived in a tarpaper shack. It was so poorly constructed that the wind literally blew through. In the winter, we stoked up the wood burning stove and huddled around it. If we left water in a glass over night, it was frozen by morning.

I was sick most of the time in that house, especially during the winter months. Mom rocked me through my fevers, sitting before the stove as the flames flickered behind its tiny isinglass window. I remember Dad coming home from work, putting his lips on my forehead to judge the intensity of my fever. He always did that when I was sick. Dad had trouble putting his love into words, but I knew he loved me then.

Somehow I survived in that house until I was three. My parents rented another house then, a twenty-four by twenty-four foot, four room bungalow that had been built only steps away from a main residence. In the spring of 1946, they bought it for a little less than $2,000. Dad made far less than a dollar an hour working every summer in the Danube Mine and logging during the winter when the mine would shut down. He had an aversion to owing anyone a cent, a trait that followed him his entire life.

I don't know how Mom and Dad swung the deal, but they did.

Chapter Five

The year my father bought the house, he also purchased twenty acres of land about a mile away. This was a prime piece of property, covered with mature aspen and three small fields. But the absolute best aspect of the property was its twenty acre frontage on a small body of water called Arvid's Lake.

As the story goes, Arvid was a farmer who lived on the opposite side of the lake from our property, long before Dad bought the land. At that time, the lake was entirely landlocked and spring fed, much deeper than it was when the property became ours.

It was a glacial lake, about fifty yards from the Mississippi River, and it was separated from the river by a high sandy ridge. As the spring fed lake kept rising, Arvid lost valuable farm land. One day, in exasperation, he dug a drainage ditch from the lake to the river. The water began to drain from the lake in a slow but steady trickle.

And then one night, according to my grandmother, the neighbors heard a terrific roar. The next morning, the community woke to see a deep cut that had been eroded between the lake and the river. The surface of the lake was some thirty feet lower than it had been the night before. Overnight, the size of Arvid's farm had increased by several acres of good, rich lake-bottom soil. Years later, thanks to Arvid, I was able to live on a small lake connected to the Mississippi by a short, shallow creek.

When I was growing up, the creek connecting the lake and the river had almost vertical banks that were more than thirty feet high, and the land surrounding Arvid's Lake sloped downward to the lake's edge like a lakebed would. In places on these sloping banks, marl—a rich, gray, crumbling soil—was mined and sold as fertilizer. The twenty acres of frontage my father bought on that little lake constituted about a third of the available shoreline.

Dad was a bull of a man. By hand, he cleared a building site on the property, cutting the aspen and jack pine, blowing stumps with dynamite, and grubbing roots. The grub hoe he used had a heavy wood handle. Its head was two-sided; one side resembled an axe blade while the other was like an extra heavy hoe.

He also dug a basement with a team of horses he borrowed from his friends, the Ingstead brothers. He hitched the team of matched Belgians to a scraper, and I watched him, wide-eyed, as he walked behind the bucket and wrestled with the handles, lifting them just enough so the sharp, leading edge dug into the soil. A thin layer of soil peeled back and collected in the scraper's belly.

Eventually, the hole became deep enough that Dad would drop down the slope from one side and emerge from it on the other with another load of dirt. With the horse reins slung over his shoulder and tied behind his back, he would guide the horses around, dump the scraper, and keep right on moving down into the hole again.

Eventually, scoop after scoop, the hole expanded until it took the shape of a basement. As I stood with my mother and watched, Dad excavated a hole six feet deep and big enough for a house, all with a scraper and a borrowed team of horses. I never heard him complain, even though he was covered with sweat that ran into his eyes and blurred his vision.

When the hole was done, the horses were returned to their owner, but the difficult job was only beginning. Dad had taken some of the trees he cut the last winter to a sawmill to be milled into one inch boards. He used the boards to build the forms for concrete basement walls. To save money, he collected large stones from farmers' fields or from along the roadsides and hauled them to our building site. Then he loaded them all by hand into a single-axle dump truck owned by a longtime friend.

Dad filled the same truck with sand that he shoveled by hand from a nearby gravel pit. The clean sand, mixed with cement and water, was used to fill a borrowed cement mixer capable of putting out a batch of cement that would nearly fill a wheelbarrow. Making a click-ety-click-ety-click-ety rhythm as it turned, the mixer produced a thick soup from the ingredients.

Dad mixed all of the concrete for our basement walls with that machine, one load at a time, and dumped the load into a wheelbarrow that had a rusted steel wheel. His muscles bulged, and the veins of his neck stood out as the wheel dug into the soft sand. He pushed his way through, over to the wooden-formed wall.

He dumped the load of mixed cement into the form, and then one by one, dropped field stones into the sloppy stuff.

Dad repeated this process in a monotonous pattern—mix the cement, dump it, and add field stones. After two or three days, maybe more, he stripped the forms away to reveal the foundation for our small, square house.

Unfortunately, our actual house still stood a mile or more away.

"Mom, what's that noise?" I asked the next morning when a sound like a huge clawing animal came from under the floor.

She assured me it was okay and then took me outside to see what the workers were doing. "See, they're pushing those big beams under the house," she told me. "That was the noise you heard. It's nothing to be afraid of."

"But why are they doing that?" My four year old mind was concerned.

"Just watch them. They're going to lift our house up and put it on a truck."

I watched in amazement, and with a little fear, as the men set timbers under the floor joists, placed four huge jacks under their ends, and then began lifting the house off its foundation.

"How are we going to get in the door?" I asked Mom in dismay as I looked up at my house, now some six feet off the ground.

"Don't worry," Mom laughed. "Dad will be home soon to help. It's going to be fun.

I watched as the movers rolled massive wheeled dollies under the beams and gently lowered them. They hooked a truck tractor onto the wheels and pulled my house down the driveway, across a small field, and parked it beside the country road.

I stood in the doorway of my home and stared out across the dusty road. Perched high up off the ground, I slept in the house that night with my parents.

The next morning, the truck began a slow journey to the new basement and foundation. There was no need to worry about power or telephone lines; we had no electricity or phone.

Later that day, the house was slid onto its new foundation. The hole was backfilled—by hand of course, with a number two, long-handled shovel—and I was home.

Chapter Six

Our house had four square rooms, each the same size and hardly bigger than oversize bathrooms. The rooms were arranged around one central closet. Each was connected to the other by a door, so we could walk in a circle from the kitchen, to the living room, to the kids' bedroom, to my parents' bedroom, and then back to the kitchen. After my sister was born, when we were older, it made for a good raceway to play tag.

"If I have to tell you kids one more time to stop running, you're going outside," Mom said through clenched teeth. "I don't care if it's snowing out!"

We'd calm down until I caught my sister, Janice, scribbling in one of my Zane Grey novels again. Then, it would be off to the races. I still have books bearing her four-year-old signature of squiggly pencil lines.

Our kitchen might have made it into *Better Homes and Gardens* magazine as a negative example of architecture. I would come in from playing, sweaty and thirsty, but there was no ice water in the refrigerator. In fact, there was no refrigerator. That meant I had to go to the sink, except there was no faucet.

Instead, I would grab the handles of the cistern pump bolted to the kitchen countertop, its lip jutting out over the single tub sink fixed into the counter. Unfortunately, the pump always lost its prime, and so if the last person to use the pump hadn't left a cup of water standing near by, I'd be pretty much out of luck.

I poured the cup of water down the top of the pump. Then I raised the handle. One stroke down, nothing came out. Up and down again. Still nothing. Up, and down, faster this time, and a thin stream of water trickled into the sink. By the fourth pull, the trickle gushed.

"Dennis, get your face out from under that spout!" Mom warned. "You don't drink water that way in my house."

But nothing felt better than to stick my face under the stream of cold groundwater and let it wash over half my head. I slurped until my belly sloshed when I moved. My joy lasted until Mom grabbed my ear, or I got tired of pumping.

The plumbing under the sink was a five gallon pail set directly beneath the drain, and woe to the person who didn't check to see if it was full and ran waste water over the floor.

One day when I was little, Mom and Dad invited Max and Pearl, long time friends, to come for dinner. I had to go to the bathroom, really bad.

Mom said, "Dennis, just open the cabinet door and go in the pail." I did, but as I started to tinkle in the bucket, Max pulled out a pocket knife.

"Here, gimme that thing, I'll cut it off," he said with a chuckle.

I kept clear of Max and his pocket knife after that.

Sewage disposal meant carrying the pail to the adjoining woods and giving its contents the old heave-ho.

Hot water was a different matter.

"Dennis, would you pump water into the tea kettle for me and put it on the stove?"

After a few minutes on the left side, the smaller side of the stove where a wood fire burned, Mom removed the steaming kettle and took it to the sink. She tipped it and poured the hot water she needed.

The linoleum on the kitchen floor was worn to match the tired wallpaper, and the frayed curtains at the windows complimented the ragged-edged hand towel hanging from the ring on the cupboard door. The towel had been washed so many times that the colors were faded, and the print was almost invisible. Though old, everything was spotless, cleaned with scalding water heated in a metal pail on top of the wood burner.

I can still picture Mom on her hands and knees each day, scrubbing with a hand-held bristled brush, wisps of her brown hair sticking to the back of her neck. Beads of sweat formed on her brow. Mom had no vacuum cleaner, but everything was wiped down with a moist rag. I don't remember her ever wearing anything but a print housedress with anklets and flat soled shoes, sensible attire for the work she did.

Years later, after Mom and Dad moved to the small town of Coleraine, Mom's home had a kitchen with a tile floor. At least once a year she bought new curtains. Her linen closet was stacked with piles of new, fluffy towels, and not one had a ragged edge.

Only a few months before Mom died of complications from cancer, my sister was going to mop the floor of Mom's modern kitchen with a long-handled sponge mop. Mom grabbed it from Janice, put it in the cupboard, took out her bristled hand brush, and got down on her hands and knees. She was wearing stylish clothes then, neat fitting slacks and a button-up blouse. She had on new sandals, was wearing her favorite perfume, and had just come from the beauty parlor.

"If you're not going to do it right, don't do it at all," she scolded.

Then she scrubbed the floor while Janice watched.

Chapter Seven

In our living room, I'd lie in front of the Junger's fuel oil fired space heater, the only means of heat for the house. There, the world and time stood still, and I'd let my imagination run wild, carried away by my books.

The stove was backed up against the wall of the closet that formed the central core to our house. It had a tiny, square window, and the flame flickered behind it, casting muted shadows on the walls.

The living room itself was quite bare. It had only two small windows, so it was dark and shadowy. The curtains were threadbare from age and sooty from the wood range in the kitchen and the space heater. Mom struggled to maintain a couple of well-used cloth covered chairs and an old sofa. She sewed slipcovers that always bunched up, and true to their name, slipped off, and she habitually smoothed and adjusted them every time she walked by.

Two faded and outdated pictures hung on the wall. One was a still life of a vase filled with cut flowers. The other was a worn out landscape, a watercolor of a harbor near Mom's father's childhood home in Devonshire, England. My grandfather had brought it with him when he came to the States in the late 1800s, at the age of sixteen. It had been water damaged when Grandma made him hang it in their leaky porch. Mom had taken the picture with her when she left home, cleaned it up the best she could, and hung it on our wall.

Like the rest of our house, the living room floor was covered with old linoleum. The finish had been worn off and, in places, the bare wood of the sub-floor was exposed. These areas were dirt traps: impossible to keep clean. On her hands and knees, Mom scraped and teased at the worn edges, coaxing out dirt from hidden crevices.

For me, the living room was a sanctuary. I remember the day I first read a written word. I was curled up on the living room floor, rested on one of the chairs while I looked at the comics in the Sunday paper. It was early winter of my first grade year, and the space heater was kicking out its BTU's. With no forewarning, I realized that I understood what was written in the bubble issuing from the mouth of Lil' Abner.

"Mom! Dad! I just read the comic strip! I can read!"

Mom was in the kitchen, and from around the corner I heard her say, "That's nice. Now wash your hands for lunch."

Dad looked up from his sports page. "I guess I don't have to read them to you anymore," he said.

Soon, I was reading anything I could lay my hands on. Our cozy living room became my refuge whenever I wanted to escape to the forest or the prairie, the sea or the mountains. I was led there by authors such as Jack London and Zane Grey. The living room was the place where I could curl up in a corner and dream about being a woodsman, or better yet, a Native American. In our cramped living quarters, finding a private space was difficult, but I could get lost in my books.

Mom worked to keep our house a home. Every spring, she bought flower seeds and planted them in our yard. Her father, Grandpa Burns, was a wonderful gardener, and his hedges and flower beds resembled those of his native England. Mom planted cosmos and nasturtiums along the house, pinks and bachelor buttons in an old tire filled with dirt, and hollyhocks by the shed. The flowers always grew with promise, especially when the spring rains filtered down, but by dry midsummer they were withered and dead. Mom would pick the few hardy blooms that did make it and arrange them in a vase to decorate the living room. She picked wild flowers, and the attar of roses filled the humble room. In the autumn, she placed cattails in a vase on a shelf.

Once when Mom was doing her best to get the living room polished, she bumped the dried cattails. Without a sound, they exploded into a hundred-million downy seeds.

Mom stared at the mess for an instant. Then she swept the vase off the shelf with her broom and beat the cattails mercilessly into the linoleum floor.

"Damn this place! Damn him! Damn my life!" she cried. "I just can't live like this anymore." She swung the broom again and again. Then she sat in the middle of the floor, her frustrations filling the air like the cattail fluff. Her body shook as she wept into her hands.

I stood in the doorway, unsure what to do. Then I picked up the shards of broken vase and tried to piece them together.

Mom remained on the floor. After several minutes, I tiptoed over to her and put my arms around her neck.

"Just go out and play, Dennis," she said tiredly. Then she got up and cleaned the living room.

We never had cattails in the house again.

Chapter Eight

With four people living in a four room house, sleeping arrangements were a bit complicated.

"You have to share your room with your sister, and that's that," Mom told me. "She's too old to sleep with Dad and me anymore, so stop your bellyaching and help me take apart this bed."

That evening, we drove into town to answer a newspaper ad: "For Sale—Bunk beds, good condition, mattresses included, $4.00." The ad had been placed by a lady whose children had outgrown the beds, and Mom and Dad went into her house to examine their condition. After they bought the beds, we tied the mattresses on the top of the car and the bedsteads and springs onto the passenger side, resting them on the car's running board.

When we got home from Grand Rapids, Dad was cranky. "You kids stop messing around. Get out of the way so I can get these beds put together," he demanded. A little later we heard him grumble, "Damn! I lost one of the bolts that holds the end on. I'll get one from the mine tomorrow." He turned on my mother as though she had lost the piece of hardware. "Gen, lift that end up on the post."

"I can't," she snapped back.

Dad rolled his eyes at the ceiling. "Why not?" he demanded.

"It's too heavy for me to lift that high."

"You're some help," Dad grouched. "Get out of the way. I'll do it alone, like I usually do."

"It isn't tight. Just look how it wiggles," Mom said once the beds were up. "Everything you do is half done, Ed. You'd better bring that bolt home tomorrow. I'm not letting the kids sleep in it this way another night."

Janice and I loved to play on those bunks. If we hung a blanket from the top bed so it draped down to the lower, the enclosed space became a tent, a cave, or the inside of a ship.

Janice had long blond hair, and she wore it down most of the time. Mom kept it sparkling clean and sometimes tied it up with ribbons into two ponytails. One rainy day, Janice and I had to stay inside because of the weather, and to vent her unspent energy, my sister was bouncing vigorously on her bed, the lower bunk. Naturally her hair would fly up when she reached the apogee of her bounce, and then she would free-fall onto her bed. On about her sixth bounce, her long hair caught in the bedsprings of the bunk above. She came back to earth, but her hair remained wound up in the spring. As she lay on her back, there before her eyes dangled a clump of hair at least an inch in diameter.

For several seconds she did nothing but stare at the clump. Then she let out a wail. Eventually, Janice calmed down enough so Mom could assess the damage, which turned out to be minimal. I don't know what hurt worse: my sister's scalp, or her vanity.

At first, it felt good to be tucked into my upper berth on a frigid winter night. The space heater in the middle of the house provided ample heat that would rise to the ceiling. While the floor of the house was cool, the space above my bunk was toasty. In the middle of the night, however, the air near the ceiling turned stifling. It was terribly dry, and the inside of my mouth and nose became cracked and irritated. To seek relief, I took my bedding down to the floor, climbing over the end of the bed in the dark. I tiptoed into the living room and lay in front of the stove.

The small mica window in the stove gave off a warm glow of light, creating figures that danced on the dark walls. I'd lie on the floor and dream I was in the wilderness with a campfire burning to keep me warm and protecting me from dangerous animals that peered at me from the surrounding darkness. My mind would wander until I wasn't sure what was real and what was just a dream.

I raise my rifle and place the front sight just behind the shoulder of the huge buck. Slowly I pull the trigger, and the buck drops in its tracks. That's when I see her, Sharon, the prettiest freckle-faced girl in my second grade class, watching me with admiration.

I walk through the woods, silently following the faint trail of bent grass and bruised leaves. The forest is deadly silent, and I know there is danger everywhere. Suddenly, there she is, Carol Jean, the prettiest blond-haired girl in my second grade class, huddled by a tree, tears running down her face. I take her hand and lead her to safety.

I am by a river. I hear screams and rush upstream. She is far out in the fast current: Karen, the prettiest brown-haired girl in my second grade class, drowning. I leap into the water and pull her to safety.

Sometimes I would just in front of the burner and watch the flames, letting their flickering mesmerize me. Other times I'd construct machines in my head: if this gear turned this way, then that gear would turn the opposite, and the third in the sequence would turn the same direction as the first, and so on until gears were spinning every which way in my mind. The final gear would end with a definite spin.

I invented things, too. There was an ice boat I planned to make using an old door, homemade runners, and a poplar pole for a mast. Or the motorbike that used the old one-lung engine behind the garage, the one that didn't run.

Finally, my mind would shut down, and I'd go to sleep

Chapter Nine

In the morning when I got up and ran to the kitchen, I could go in one of two directions: through the living room or through my parents' bedroom. I usually chose their bedroom, the closer route to the back door.

I'd race out onto the back steps. There was nothing more satisfying after a night's sleep than standing to face the woods, gazing out over the garden, and peeing off the back porch.

"Dennis, it's only fifty feet to the outhouse. Use it."

But by that time it was already too late.

Our outhouse was well designed. It had air holes under the eaves for good ventilation and to let in enough sunshine to read by, and the hole dug under the structure was deeper than most. Dad was a good digger.

I'd walk, sometimes run, down the path to it, breaking off a small branch on the way. I'd open the door, go over to my favorite hole, and swish the branch around a couple of times. This cleaned away the spider webs and any insects that might be lurking below the seat.

The building was only big enough to stand and turn around in, and a board shelf, just about seat level, ran across the back wall. Two holes were cut in it: one to fit large fannies, the other to fit smaller ones. I was ambi-fannied when it came to choosing.

On either side of the holes sat a Sears Roebuck or Montgomery Ward catalogue. I passed the time by paging through these and dreaming of buying a shotgun, a set of animal traps, or even a fishing rod. Sometimes I'd find a copy of last Sunday's newspaper, and that was prime print, especially if the comic section was still available. The sports section belonged to Dad. By the end of the week, he had pretty well memorized all of the baseball statistics.

I think my reading ability jumped up a grade level because of our outhouse.

Eventually the catalogue or newspaper ceased to be reading material and became essential. The catalogues had a few pages that were glossy, but most were low quality paper without a shiny finish. I'd tear out one of these, ball it up in a tight mass, unfold it, and ball it up again, repeating the process several times until the page became soft and pliable. This toilet paper option was better than the corn cobs one of my friends had to use.

When it rained, I ran fast so I didn't have to shiver over the hole while the water evaporated from my hair and clothing. In the winter, I wouldn't lower my pants all the way. I kept them wrapped around my thighs to stay warm. I didn't do much reading in the winter.

Chapter Ten

Bath night was an event at our house.

"Dad's getting the tub," Mom would announce. "Take out your braids, Janice. It's your turn first."

Dad brought in our new tub and placed it in the middle of the kitchen floor. The three foot oval trough shined through its galvanized surface and waited for us to fill it. I pumped cold water, filling a three gallon pail from the spout, and I dumped it into the tub. I pumped and dumped until the tub was about one-quarter full.

"Fill two more pails for me, and then you can go out and play for a while," Mom commanded, and I'd bolt outside as soon as I was done.

She put the last two pails of water to heat on the stove, and when the water was boiling, she wrestled them down and mixed them with the cold water already in the tub. Then Janice got in, and Mom scrubbed until my sister was spotless. Dirt had no chance when Mom attacked.

"Dennis, it's your turn now," Mom shouted from the kitchen door to where I was digging at the edge of our driveway. "You don't want to bathe in cold water." Never mind that the water was already dirty from my sister's bath.

"Don't forget to wash your ears, and be sure to scrub your feet," Mom dictated once she'd coaxed me into the tub. "I'll be in to check you after I comb out Janice's hair." When she came into the kitchen a few minutes later, Mom was a drill sergeant ready for inspection. My ears were never clean enough, and so the washcloth was soaped again and wormed into my ears until I felt like one of those cartoon characters who put the cloth in one side and pulled it out the other. She would scrub my feet, especially my right foot that had a few faint freckles on the instep, first with the washcloth and then with a brush until the skin was pink.

When I was an adult, I was walking barefoot in my mother's house, and she noticed the dark brown speckles on my right foot. The freckles had darkened as I got older.

"That's a birthmark?" she asked, shocked. "I spent the first eight years of your life trying to scrub it off!"

There was another bathing ritual enjoyed by many of the families in Blackberry: the weekly sauna. A sauna was one of the first buildings erected when a Finnish family established a farm. Many times the family lived in it until a larger home could be built. Although it was sometimes used as a birthing room, its main purpose was always for bathing.

"You kids get some clean clothes to bring with, and don't forget a towel. We're going over to Erholtz's," Mom announced one Friday night. "They have the sauna heated up and asked if we wanted to come for a bath."

I scrambled to get ready, happy I didn't have to scrunch into the galvanized tub full of tepid, dirty water.

When we got there, the sauna was already heated.

"You and Dad go in first. Janice and I will take the second shift," Mom said. "Don't forget to wash your feet, Dennis. Eddie, make sure he washes his feet."

I walked into the dressing room and smelled the combined aroma of wet cedar, birch twigs, warm bar soap, burning wood, and steam. After Dad and I stripped naked, he opened the door to the sauna stove and slipped in a couple pieces of split firewood. The stove was built into the wall separating the dressing room from the steam room, and it could be stoked from the dressing room side. That way, the place where we bathed didn't get dirty from hauling in wood.

Dad opened the door between the two rooms, and I gingerly tiptoed in. The steam room was small, just large enough to hold a half-dozen people if they didn't sit too far apart. On the far wall were three benches that rose up the wall like stairs. The wood stove protruded into the room, and a steel crib on top was filled with small, wave-polished lake stones the size of chicken eggs. It was hot as a frying pan.

I took my seat on the lowest bench, and Dad moved right to the top, the hottest seat. On the lowest bench, the sweat began to ooze out of my pores. Up high, the sweat poured off Dad.

"Okay now, son, I'm going to put water on the rocks," he warned. "If you have to, get down on the floor."

He took a small ladle of water from a bucket and threw it on the rocks. The water hissed and sputtered, and the steam rolled up in clouds. Two or three ladles-full, and the place was thick with fog and hot enough to cook lobster.

My lungs burned, and I got down on the floor. The floor was made of wood boards spaced just far enough apart to allow water to seep through the cracks. The boards were planed smooth to begin with, and after years of soap and water washing over them, they were like silk against my hot cheek. I sucked in cooler air from near the floor. Girding myself as in an initiation to manhood, I returned to the first bench. When I was more accustomed to the heat, I moved up to the second. I wondered if I could go all the way up. Dad was up there, and he wasn't keeling over.

I decided to risk it. I climbed to the last level and sat next to Dad, feeling much older than I really was. By then, the steam had dissipated.

"Why don't you move down to the floor again," Dad suggested. "I want one more dose of steam." He lifted up the ladle and threw another splash of water on the hot rocks. Then, he picked up a hand-sized bundle of birch twigs that had been standing in the corner.

What in the heck is Dad going to do with those? I thought to myself. I didn't think I'd done anything wrong, so I was startled when he began to gently swat me with them, first across my back, then on my legs and across my chest and shoulders. Strangely enough, it felt pretty good. Then he swatted himself, only harder than he'd swatted me.

Eventually, we took bars of soap, some strongly perfumed kind, and lathered up. I scrubbed my feet really well.

"Stand still now," Dad said. "I'm going to dump a pail of water over you to rinse down. Keep your eyes closed so you don't get soap in them." He poured tepid water over my head. Then he rinsed himself.

When stepped out into the dressing room, a wave of fresh summer air made me shiver. We toweled off and donned our clothes. I inhaled, and it seemed that even the insides of my lungs were clean.

The evening was not quite over. Up at the house, the hostess had prepared a light lunch of coffee, cheese, crackers, and something sweet for us, and we sipped cold water to replace the liquid we had lost from all the sweating.

True Finns had a ritual they followed after the rinse, just before they toweled off and got dressed. If they could, they built their sauna near a lake or stream so they could dash out of the sauna and dive into cold water. I had friends who, in the winter, would leap out of the sauna and roll in the snow. Some even made snow angels while they were in the buff, leaving artistic silhouettes behind.

A lot of problems were talked out and solved in the sauna. It's difficult to take yourself too seriously when you're sitting naked in front of your close friends and relatives.

Chapter Eleven

With the installation of electric transmission lines into the country, life became easier in some ways but more complicated in others. The power grids were not terribly dependable, and power outages were the norm, especially during electrical storms like the one that raged outside only weeks after they'd run a power line to our house. A tree had toppled over the transmission line, and Mom sent us scurrying to find pre-electricity appliances. "Dennis, where did you put the lantern? Sit where you are while I find the matches and get some candles lit."

When the candles were burning, the room took on a shadowy glow like what came from our space heater, but a bit brighter.

"Did you find the lantern?" Mom asked with a little quiver in her voice. "Take it into the basement and look for one of the old kerosene lamps. Be careful on the rickety stairs."

I cautiously descended into the black abyss where there were no handrails to catch me if I slipped, brushing away cobwebs so they didn't drag across my face. I expected a slimy hand to grab my shoulder at any time. Eventually, I raced up the steep stairs to safety, clutching the kerosene lamp.

"It doesn't have any kerosene in it," Mom said with disappointment. "I wonder if I can use the fuel oil from that can in the shed. I'll bet Mae will know."

The telephone company had hooked up our phone line about the same time the power went in, so when Dad worked the afternoon or night shift, Mom could call her neighbors in an emergency.

She lifted the receiver.

"Number, please," the operator asked.

"Six-O-Four-J-Three, please," Mom said, and the connection was made to our neighbor down the road. "Mae, our lights are out, how about yours?" Mom listened to Mae's answer, and then went on. "Eddie is working tonight, and we've got kerosene lamps, but no kerosene. Do you think it would be okay to use fuel oil?"

Before Mae could even form the words to answer, the party at Six-O-Four-J-Six, blurted into the phone. "Oh Lord! You can't do that. It will blow up!"

There was a long moment of silence. Six-O-Four-J-Six was an elderly lady, Mrs. Elgin, who lived near the highway. She was notorious for rubbernecking, listening in on calls made to others on the party line. Then she would pass on the news to other gossips. She knew she had made an etiquette blunder and quickly tried to wriggle her way out. "I just picked up the phone to make a call myself, when I heard you ask that question, Gen. It's a good thing I happened to pick up just at that instant, because you might have burned your house down. That's what I call fate, I guess."

Such were the trials of being on a party line.

Just about everyone on our road was connected to that same line, not to mention a few families who lived on another road. The phone numbers started with Six-O-Four-J-One and ran up to at least Six-O-Four J-Eight.

To make a call, I'd lift the receiver, place it to my ear, and wait for the operator to ask for the number. Somewhere, probably in Grand Rapids, was a switchboard, and the operator would manually make the connection between the caller's phone and the recipient.

This type of service provided much more than just phone connections. In response to "Number, please," I could say, "Would you give me the correct time, please?" And the operator would respond with the time. Or I might call information and ask for the address of so and so.

Of course not everyone had a phone in those days. Recently, at an antique store, I bought a phone book from 1937 that had only three Blackberry Township numbers listed. One I recognized as Mae's father-in-law, Solomon Erholtz. I was also surprised to find that the Blackberry School had its own number, Twelve-F-Thirteen. Back then all of the numbers in the Grand Rapids exchange fit on eight pages. The book for the entire Iron Range from Biwabik to Grand Rapids was less than half an inch thick.

Mom couldn't call her parents in Keewatin because they had no phone. But if she wanted to talk to her dad, she could call where he worked.

"Eddie, I'm going to call Pa. Is that okay?"

"Okay. But make sure you call person to person. And watch the time," he reminded her. "The last time you went over three minutes, and it cost a week's pay." Dad exaggerated to make his point.

Mom lifted the receiver on our phone and heard the operator's voice.

"Number, please."

"I'd like the Keewatin Exchange please."

"What number do you wish?"

"One-O-Five-W, please."

"Do you wish station to station, or person to person?"

"Person to person, please."

Then she heard the phone ringing: one ringy-dingy, two ringy-dingys, three ringy-dingys.

"Lerch Brothers Incorporated," the receptionist at the other end answered.

"I have a person to person call for a Mr. William Burns," the operator asked. "Is he in?"

"No, I'm sorry; Mr. Burns isn't working today," the party at Lurch Brothers answered.

"Thank you," the operator politely said.

Mom heard the receptionist at Lurch Brothers hang up the phone, and the operator came on the line. "I'm sorry. Mr. Burns wasn't available to take your call."

"Thank you operator, for your time," Mom said.

"You're welcome, and have a nice day," was the operator's pleasant reply.

Because Mom's Pa wasn't available to talk, she wasn't charged for the call.

Back then, people actually spoke to people on the phone when they called information rather than to a computer located in some distant city. Perhaps that is why when I dial information and a computerized voice asks, "Information for what city?" I still answer, "Remer, Minnesota, please," as if the computer cares whether I say "please."

Station to station calls were always billed, no matter who answered. Had Mom called her Pa station to station, she would have had to pay to speak to a secretary at Lurch Brothers. Naturally, it cost more for person to person calls.

Calls were expensive, and Dad had a right to be concerned if we went over the three minute limit. According to my 1937 phone book, the first three minutes of a station to station call from Blackberry to Keewatin cost twenty-five cents. However, person to person for the same call cost thirty-five cents for three minutes. Minutes over the initial three were billed at an even higher rate. Dad only made about four dollars a day.

When she made local calls, several things could happen, all equally annoying. Mom would no sooner be connected to her party than the phone would begin to click. Click—click, click, click, click, clickclickclickclick. This was to let her know that someone else on our party line wanted to use the phone. If she ignored the clicking, someone would interrupt. "Can I please use the phone? This is an emergency!" The emergency was usually something like a neighbor wanting to talk to Grandma-So-and-So about a recipe.

Or, she might hear a muffled sneeze, and not from the person to whom she was speaking. If she didn't hang up immediately after she said goodbye, she'd hear a series of clicks as the neighbors up and down the line hung up their phones. There were few secrets in Blackberry.

Chapter Twelve

The addition of electricity to our home meant that we stopped living in 1890 mode and moved up to at least 1920.

At that time, Dad also bought a propane-gas kitchen range for Mom to cook on. Our old wood burning kitchen range worked well, but it made summers brutal for Mom. All of the canning and preserving had to be done during the summer, along with cooking the regular meals. In August, when the outside temperature sweltered, the interior of our house was miserable to work in with the added heat of a wood burner. Mom might as well have been in a sauna. She didn't even have a way to make ice cubes for a cold drink of water.

Mom was overjoyed when Dad brought home the new, shiny-white gas range. "Oh Eddie," she gushed in a moment of joy. "It's wonderful. Look how clean it is, and look at the size of the oven! I think I can fit three loaves of bread in there at once. Can you believe the burners all have pilot lights?" I never saw her so happy.

Not too long after that, our refrigerator was delivered, which changed my life in big ways. Up until then, Mom would say each night at dinner, "Young man, you won't leave this table until you drink your milk."

"Aw Mom, you know I can't stand warm milk," I balked.

"Hush now. You need the calcium."

I'd start to drink, but I'd gag.

"Drink it, Dennis. It's not that bad."

"But it tastes funny," I'd complain, my nose wrinkled up at the smell. "I'm going to throw up if I have to drink it."

If I was lucky, Mom would take a sip and spit it out. "Darn. It's sour already. I just picked it up from Anderson's yesterday! Honestly, we waste more milk around here." Then I'd be off the hook.

When the refrigerator came and I was served ice cold milk for the first time, it put an end to the worst of our battles.

Before the refrigerator, we bought ice cream by the pint at the Blackberry Store, rushed home before it became strawberry-cream soup, and ate it as fast as we could. After, we had ice cream on demand. We bought it by the quart and saved some for the next day.

The refrigerator's freezing compartment was minuscule. It had enough room for our quart of ice cream, two ice cube trays, a pound of hamburger, and a ring of sausage.

Our three-sided back porch served as our deep freeze from late November to early March. After deer season, Dad hung a quarter or two of venison from spikes pounded in two-by-four studs. Mom set out a pot or a casserole container with leftovers from supper. When she baked cookies, they were wrapped in wax paper and placed in a tin so mice couldn't get them.

There were two problems with that plan. Every winter had one or more surprise thaws. When that happened, our stockpile was in jeopardy of thawing and spoiling.

The second problem involved wild animals. One deer season Dad shot a fat buck and shared it with the neighbor who hadn't gotten one. Dad laid the half-carcass in our freezer-entryway and came in to eat supper before he processed the venison.

After supper he went out to retrieve the side of venison but returned empty handed. He headed for the phone in a rush. "Hi, Vic? I wonder if you could come over and help me," Dad said, agitated. "I left the half of that buck on the porch, and when I went back out, it was gone. Looks like wolf tracks in the snow or a pretty big dog." There was silence on our end while Dad listened. "Thanks, Vic," he finally said. "I need that half and won't get another legal chance this year. See you in ten minutes. Bring a good light if you have one—and your rifle with open sights."

Dad and Vic tracked the animal for hours that night, but they never did catch up with it. When the tracks disappeared into a deep ravine covered with raspberry and blackberry brambles, they decided to give up the chase. That winter we lived without venison.

Once we had a refrigerator and a gas stove, Mom completed her trifecta when she finally got a dasher type washing machine with an electric motor and a set of clothes ringers mounted to its side.

Some of our neighbors had older washing machines rusting away behind the outbuildings on their farms. Instead of electric motors, they had been powered by small gasoline engines which were a real pain to start once the machine aged a little. It seemed they always needed a new spark plug or to have the gas line cleaned. Having an electric powered washer was a real timesaver for any family.

I don't remember Mom talking much when she washed clothes. It's hard to talk and haul three-gallon pails of water down a flight of steep basement stairs. By the time we got the new washing machine, our hand operated cistern pump had been replaced by a shallow-well electric pump in the basement. Although there was a cold-water tap down there, Mom still had to run water upstairs, put it on the stove to boil, and then carry it downstairs and dump it into the machine.

After the clothes had sloshed around in the machine, I watched Mom take them out one at a time and feed them through the two wringers. The wringers were mounted one above the other, and the tension could be adjusted by hand to accommodate heavier or lighter loads.

Because Mom was so isolated in the country, she talked to me like she would an adult. "These wringers are really dangerous," she said one washing day. "I heard of a woman who got her fingers stuck, and it pulled her whole arm in before she could get to the switch and shut it off. This thing scares the bejeebers out of me. I've heard of women getting too close to the wringers while they were bending over and getting a breast caught in the wringer. I can't think of anything more horrible." She paused. "I suppose that is where the saying, 'One tit in the ringer,' comes from." She gave a nervous laugh.

Luckily, our washing days passed without incident. Mom wrung the soap-filled clothes, drained the washer's tub, and filled it with cold rinse water from the tap next to the machine. Then she repeated the wringing process one more time. Finally the clean, wet clothes were carried upstairs and outside. Winter or summer, Mom had to hang the clothes on the line. In the summer, the sun and wind fluffed and dried them.

In the winter, the sheets, towels, and underwear froze solid. After a few hours of that cold treatment, Mom would bring the clothes in. She stood the pants up against the wall behind the heater and laid out shirts and towels across beds, chairs, and counters. When the laundry became limp, it was remarkably dry and smelled as fresh as if it had been blown dry by a summer's breeze.

Chapter Thirteen

Little by little, life in the country changed as we caught up with technology. Even so, life remained strenuous for Mom. She was a small woman, but she toiled day after day lifting loads she shouldn't have, cleaning our porous and dusty house, and cooking meals. In her spare time, she patched our pants and darned the holes in our socks. By the time she was twenty-six, when I was six years old, Mom was tired, discouraged, and desperate to get out of Blackberry.

But I was so busy enjoying living the country life that I was unaware of Mom's despair. Even something as simple as a radio program filled me with amazement.

"And now, sponsored by Ajax, the foaming cleanser, we present *Old Ma Perkins,*" the voice from the radio announced. Dramatic music began to play, and a narrator intoned the virtues of this grand old lady in his polished baritone voice.

Then, it was commercial time and a trio sang a ditty: "So use Ajax, the foaming cleanser, foams the dirt right down the drain."

This jingle was followed by a glub, glub, glub sound effect.

The music sped up when a character was running and slowed down and become soft when a woman was speaking. Deep and ominous strains played when the hero was in danger. Violin music meant love was in the air.

I would rush to the radio after school to listen to my favorite program, *Straight Arrow.* Straight Arrow was a Native American who spoke a broken parody of the way my friends and I thought a real Native would speak. As his name implied, he was brave, intelligent, and honest beyond reproach. He was everything I wanted to be. I'd be on the edge of the kitchen counter beside the radio, engrossed, when the show began.

"We leave Straight Arrow hanging by his fingers from the cliff edge so we can hear a word from our sponsor," the announcer informed us. "When we return, we'll find out if this is the end of our hero, or if he will escape through his cunning and wiles."

"Kids, do you want to have the strength of Straight Arrow?" the commercial began. "You can, you know. Eat the right foods, drink plenty of milk, and exercise. The right foods include a good breakfast, and what better breakfast is there than Nabisco Shredded Wheat? Eat it cold, or have Mom pour boiling water over it for a delicious, nutritious hot meal. And, as a special bonus, in each box of Nabisco Shredded Wheat, you get two *Straight Arrow* collector cards. Learn the secrets of our hero, and you can be like him, too.

"Remember kids, have your mom buy Nabisco Shredded Wheat. No other brand will do."

By this time Straight Arrow's fingers were getting pretty tired as he clung to the edge of the cliff. Finally, he was able to swing himself up to race into the woods and safety. He survived to act another day.

I lived for those *Straight Arrow* cards. Each one held a bit of Native American lore that I believed to be absolute truth. I desperately wanted to be Native American. I studied cards that taught how to track wild animals, how to survive in the wilderness with only a hunting knife, or how to withstand extreme temperatures. I ate enough shredded wheat to fill the haymow of a barn.

Dad enjoyed listening to boxing matches. Sometimes he and my uncle Bill would sit by the radio with a jar of pickled pigs' knuckles and a couple of beers between them. My uncle would duck and dodge the punches as they were described by the announcer. "That's it, hit 'im again! Ya got 'im on the ropes; now finish 'im off. Ah, ya let 'im slip away, ya bum!"

Mom and Aunt Margaret would have coffee and goodies in the kitchen while the fight was on. Dad came to sit at the table, but my uncle wouldn't leave the living room.

"Come on ya bum, get off the mat!" he'd shout. "What's wrong with ya, ya got a glass chin?"

By the end of the fight, Uncle Bill was as exhausted as the boxers.

There were certain programs I would listen to only when all of the lights were on and my family was in the same room. One of these programs was *The Shadow*. Ominous organ music would play, and the sound of a creaking door emanated from the radio. The hair on the back of my neck stood up as the narrator spoke:

"What evil lurks in the hearts of men? The Shadow knows." He gave a sinister and mocking laugh.

At that point, I turned the radio off. I never found out what it was The Shadow knew.

Chapter Fourteen

"Look at what Grandma gave me!" I exclaimed as I opened my Christmas presents the winter I was eight. "It's a book about Indians. And look at these pictures inside! This is perfect."

I had been given the book *Indians of North America*, written by Holling C. Hollings. Since I wanted to be a Native American, it became my prize possession. The hero in each was a boy or a girl who accomplished something remarkable for the tribe. When I escaped to my world in the woods, I emulated what I read about.

The book said Indian boys toughened themselves by seeing how long they could sit motionless alone in the woods. No matter what, they would sit still for hours. Of course, I tried to see how long I could sit without moving.

Holy cow, the mosquitoes are really thick today. There must be fifty of them on my arms alone. I'm not going to move; I'm not going to move; I'm not going to move.

Regardless of the mosquito bites, the time I spent sitting in the woods, preparing myself to become an "Indian Brave" did have its rewards. Through observation, I learned to identify animals.

"Did you see that gopher run across the road?"

"Mom, that wasn't a gopher. It was a chipmunk," I'd correct.

"Come on, how could you tell that?" Mom would ask, disbelieving. "It was so far away, all I could make out was its shape. How can you be so sure of yourself?"

"Chipmunks run with their tails held in the air. Gophers run with their tail dragging behind," I'd tell her expertly. "That one's tail was up. It was a chipmunk."

For Christmas when I was seven, my parents gave me a real bow and arrow. It was made out of polished lemon wood, and it could send an arrow clean through a cardboard box.

"Let me show you how to string it," Dad said, taking up my gift. "Put your knee inside the curve, like this. Now slide the loop of the string up into the groove on the end. The guy at the store said to keep it unstrung when you aren't using it. If you don't, it'll lose its spring."

"Listen to your father now," Mom admonished. "He talked to the man about how to handle this. And be careful. I'm afraid you're going to put your eye out with that thing."

That Christmas, I also received a half-dozen arrows along with a leather quiver from my aunt Bertha. It had fancy beadwork on it which I was sure was authentic Indian workmanship.

I shot hundreds and hundreds of shots with my present that winter. Dad rigged up a target in the basement so I could shoot even during the coldest days. Most of the time, I shot outside, and I used the garage for a backstop. By spring, I could put the majority of my shots in the bull's-eye.

When spring did come, I headed for the woods—armed and dangerous. But my new bow presented a dilemma for me. I didn't want my BB gun to gather dust in the corner of my bedroom.

I got my BB gun the year before, when I was six. I sold garden seeds in the spring to earn a prize: my own Daisy air rifle. A few weeks after I turned in the paperwork for my sales, I received my prize. Then I roamed the forest with my trusty rifle, shooting at branches and pine cones. As I crept through the fern patches in summer or silently waded through snow in winter, I imagined a grouse sticking up its head. I would have to hit it just right to kill it. Then I'd make a triumphal entry into our home, just like the Indian boy in the picture in my book.

That's when I made my decision. The bow was more authentically Indian. The rifle was a white man's invention, so I would use my bow.

Chapter Fifteen

When Dad worked a day shift, he usually was home about four o'clock. Fortunately, my favorite radio programs were either over by that time or hadn't started, which meant I didn't have to choose between the radio and Dad.

He always came home from work covered with grease and red ore dust. He'd pull up a chair, take off his work boots, and lift me onto his lap. "Boy, I had to work hard today," he'd say. "That darn number sixteen, we can't keep a rear end in the old bugger. I took it apart today, and the ring gear was a mess of steel shavings. I just rebuilt it last month. When I got the hubs off, the planetaries were shot too. I think it's that darn Charlie. He drives like he's nuts. Then, when the truck breaks down, he gets to sit while I try to fix what he broke. One of these days he's going to hurt somebody."

I didn't understand a thing, only that Dad held me on his lap.

Most of the adult males in my family were miners. Both grandfathers worked in the mines, in addition to several uncles, including my uncle Johnny. The work wasn't pleasant. These were iron mines, and the red ore permeated every pore of Dad's body, staining him a reddish orange. No amount of bathing could remove the dye job. After Dad retired, it literally took six months for the color to work its way out.

The work was also fraught with danger, and reports of miner deaths were all too commonplace. Injuries were a regular occurrence. One day, Dad came home from work with a queasy look on his face. He sat at the kitchen table.

"Old Pete Erickson got caught in the drill rig today," he said as he drank his usual cup of coffee. "It grabbed the leg of his coverall and wound it up like a corkscrew. I brought him a jug of cold water, and he drank the whole thing while they unwound his leg. Poor devil. It had to be his good leg."

Men were often forced to perform work for which they were neither trained nor physically capable of doing. In those cases, injury or even death lurked close by.

I never knew my grandfather; he was electrocuted when the boom of the drill rig he was riding on struck an overhead high-voltage power line. Only a few days before, he had been putting up hay with Dad on the family farm.

"Tomorrow, I start a new job on the drill rig," he told Dad, who was then nineteen. "I have the weirdest feeling that I made a mistake taking it, that maybe I should have stayed with the job I had."

All Grandma received in compensation for her and her family's loss was a message of condolence from the mining company representative.

Even those who worked years in the mines without having a fatal accident usually ended up broken and bent. Dad was a mechanic for most of his working years. He maintained the large diesel trucks that were used to haul the ore from the depths of the pit, the diesel bulldozers and graders, and the yard locomotive. This machine was a diesel-electric engine that was used to move gondola cars. It pushed empties up a grade and parked them beyond the mouth of a hopper through which the processed ore could be dumped. The gondolas were released four at a time from the backed-up string and positioned to take on their load. The yard locomotive pulled them away when they were all full.

It was on that engine that Dad had a life-altering accident. Mining technology had advanced by then to where the mines could remain open year round, and Dad had enough seniority to hold a job even if there was a slowdown. It was winter, and everything was covered with ice, including the catwalk around the top of the locomotive. Dad was beginning to perform some routine maintenance on it. He was walking the catwalk when he slipped on the ice and fell.

Instinctively, as he plummeted to the ground, he reached out and caught the railing. He hung there by one arm until he could finally reach around with his other and grasp a metal support. Then he was able to swing a leg up onto the catwalk and pull himself to safety.

That night, his elbow swelled to three times its normal size. By morning, he couldn't bend it. He went to work that day, but he stopped at the office to file an accident report before he punched in. Dad asked to speak with the superintendent of the mine. I heard him tell Mom about the exchange that night.

"I fell off the yard engine yesterday, and I can't bend my elbow this morning," Dad had explained. "It's hurt pretty bad. Something pulled in my back, too. I had a hard time getting out of bed this morning."

The superintendent was unsympathetic. He said that he doubted it was as painful as Dad made it out to be, but he said to have the company doctor look at it.

The mining companies had "company doctors" under the employ of the corporations, and all injured men had to go through them if they were to gain any compensation for their injuries.

"I understand you had an accident, Mr. Herschbach," the company doctor said. "Let me take a look at it. Now try to bend it. I'll help." The doctor began to manipulate Dad's sore and swollen joint.

Dad winced with pain. "Dammit, that hurts! I came here for help, not to have you make it worse," he complained.

The doctor decided to take an X-ray of Dad's injured elbow. After that was done, he diagnosed the injury as a sprain and told Dad to go back to work in three days. The doctor said to use a hot water bottle and take aspirin until the pain subsided. Then he wrote up a report for the mine superintendent to have for his files.

In three days, Dad went back to work, and the company didn't have to pay any compensation other than for his one doctor visit. He lost three days wages.

As the years went by, Dad's back became more and more painful, and his arm, the one that had been "sprained," began to turn in a spiral so that, when his arm hung by his side, the palm of his hand faced outward. He couldn't fully extend that arm. Eventually, he became so crippled he couldn't work.

He went to a back specialist at the University Hospital, paid for and authorized by the company, and was subjected to several tests. The report came back to the mine officials: "This man is a malingerer, and I strongly doubt his willingness to work."

That cut into Dad as surly as a surgeon's knife could have.

A year later he was sent by the company to a back specialist in Duluth. That doctor said he could fuse the two injured vertebrae in Dad's back, and he guaranteed that it would be 100% successful. The doctor's report was placed in Dad's growing medical file with the company.

Dad sought advice from his family doctor in whom he placed a great deal of faith. That doctor told him not to consent to surgery until he absolutely couldn't walk. He said that back surgery was still in its infancy and that the success rate was extremely low.

At that point Dad consulted a lawyer.

"Ed, it's going to cost you a few bucks, but I want you to go to a specialist on your own dime," his lawyer advised. "Don't tell anyone you're going, and don't sign a release for your records. Have them sent to you personally. Then bring them to me."

Dad followed his lawyer's advice. Once again, he went to the University Hospital in Minneapolis. This time, however, he saw a doctor his attorney had chosen and not one hired by the mining company. The doctor looked at Dad's X-rays with surprise. "Mr. Herschbach, how did you break your elbow so badly? And why didn't you have it properly set? As for your back, your injury has degenerated to bone on bone with nerves crushed between. I am amazed you are still walking, let alone working."

When the lawyer received the specialist's report, he filed for Social Security disability for Dad, which was almost immediately granted. At their next meeting, the lawyer said it was time to go after the company. The papers were filed, and only a week later, a mining company representative from Cleveland paid Dad a visit.

"Mr. Herschbach, I'd advise you to give it up," the man said. He was dressed in an expensive suit and carried a leather briefcase. They stood in our front yard while he lectured Dad about the futility of taking on corporate. "You aren't going to beat us. I'm authorized to offer you a lump sum payment for partial disability. Take it or leave it."

Dad's lawyer went for the jugular. He contended that Dad did not want to quit working and that he would be losing years' worth of wages. Therefore, he sued for the wages Dad would lose until normal retirement age, and after that, the company would pay the difference between Dad's Social Security check and what his full pension would have been had he continued working. This would be in effect until Dad died.

Thankfully, the judge ruled in Dad's favor. The knowledge that he would no longer have to work through days of excruciating pain was a tremendous relief for him. He was fifty-five at the time, and because of his condition could not be employed at any other job. Now his future was secure.

As they left the courthouse, his lawyer put his hand on Dad's shoulder.

"Ed, I want you to go out there and live a long, long time."

Chapter Sixteen

Shortly after his accident, but years before his court ordered settlement, Dad went off to work at his usual time, six in the morning, and I slept until about seven or so. I was just sitting down to breakfast when Dad came through the door, lunch pail in hand. He sat down at the kitchen table. Mom came into the room, exasperated because the family would be without a day's wages; there was no such thing as sick pay if Dad missed a day.

"What's wrong? What in the world are we going to live on if you miss work again?" she demanded.

Dad placed his contorted face in his hands. "Johnny died!" He buried his face in his arms, and his body convulsed uncontrollably as he wept. That was the first of the few times I saw Dad cry.

Uncle John was Dad's brother-in-law. He had a heart condition and had been assigned the job classification of shovel oiler. His job was to make sure the huge electric-powered shovels had their gears lubricated and that all moving parts slipped freely past each other. It was a job that didn't require a great deal of physical exertion.

That particular morning, when Uncle John was finishing his graveyard shift (the one from eleven at night to seven in the morning), the shovel needed to be moved closer to the bank of ore. It was self-propelled, moving on cleated tracks. However, the electric power cables, thicker than a man's wrist, had to be pulled along behind.

Several men were required for this chore, which was made all the more difficult because the bottom of the mine pit was wet. This day, it was more of a quagmire than usual, and the men were up to their thighs in ochre mud.

"Hey Johnny, get your butt down here and help," the foreman yelled. "We're having a heck of a time with this cable."

"I'm an oiler," Johnny objected. "I'm not supposed to do that kind of work."

"Do you want to work or not? You sit on your hind-end all shift; you can pull for five minutes."

With that threat on his mind, Uncle John got out of the shovel's cab and waded into the mud. He died of a heart attack a few minutes later as he helped pull the heavy cable.

Dad was just coming to work the day shift, and as he drove through the pit bottom, he stopped by a group of men who were trying to revive his brother-in-law. When he realized it was too late, Dad turned around and came home.

We drove over to Uncle John's place later that morning. I had no idea what was going on, and my cousin Terry, eight years old, was walking around in a daze. Janice and I were told to stay in the car.

My cousin Terry and I had played together since we were old enough to walk. Like most of us raised in Blackberry, his parents had little money, but Terry had three older half-brothers, three older half-sisters, and two sisters. They had enough kids in the family to field a baseball team.

Dad's older sister, Marie, had married John Erholtz, and they had six children. The youngest was a baby when Marie developed leukemia and died. Dad's younger sister, Gen, helped with the motherless children. Eventually she married Johnny, and they had three children, Mary, Judy, and Terry.

That day, the three of them came to the car window. We tried to have a conversation, but all we did was look at each other in confusion. Tears streaked the dust on Terry's checks.

The image of Dad crumpled at the kitchen table remained etched in my mind forever.

For the next many years, my cousins were forced by circumstances to work the family farm while my aunt took a job in town. One day, a year after Johnny's death, Mom, Janice, and I went to my cousins' home for a visit. We walked about a mile down our country road, then turned off to cut through a neighbor's pasture. The farmer raised milk cows and had a Guernsey bull as a breeder.

"Be careful, kids," Mom said. "I'll spread the barbed wire fence so you can crawl through. Janice, watch so your hair doesn't get tangled in the barbs."

I hesitated. "Mom, is it safe? The bull's staring at us."

"He's all the way across the pasture," Mom said, trying to sound reassuring. "We'll stay right next to the fence. If he starts coming this way, we'll scoot under. Just keep your eye on him."

The bull wasn't all that far off, and his bloodshot eyes were following our every step. He began to paw the ground, sending divots of dirt flying above and behind him, but he didn't step forward. We moved a little faster because of him, and in no time, we were under the fence on the other side.

With the bull on one side of the fence and me on the other, I felt safe. We were in the cool of a scrub forest with its thickets of plum shrubs, hazelnut brush, scattered aspen, and birch. I smelled the jack pine's pungent turpentine along with the sweet fern that was growing along the trail.

Eventually, we broke into the open and walked across the stubble of the newly mowed hayfield. We trekked over another forty-acre stretch of farmland, and after a half-hour, I could finally see my cousin's house. For the first time in days, I'd have the chance to play with other kids.

"Hey, you guys want to play some baseball?" I asked my cousin Terry as soon as I saw him.

"No," Terry answered dejectedly. "Judy has to weed the strawberry patch, I have to split firewood, and Mary's picking raspberries. Arvid is working over at Erickson's, helping them put up the second crop of clover."

With their father gone, there was always something that had to be done on the farm. Only after their jobs were finished could they play like kids.

One time, when I was a couple of years older and could walk through the pasture, the woods, and cross the field alone, I went to my cousin's house. Terry was home alone, and at the age of nine, he was expected to plow the newly mowed hayfield to prepare it for the next crop. He fired up the John Deere tractor and hitched it to the two-bottom moldboard plow. Together we set off for the field, me riding on the fender, Terry driving. The two cylinders of the tractor made a characteristic, "punk, punk, punk, punk" sound.

Terry stopped at the edge of the field.

"I have to lower the plow," he shouted above noise of the engine. "Get off and give me a hand. If we both get on the lever, we can do it." I helped him push back on the three-foot long lever to take the tension off the retainer pin. Terry squeezed the release with one hand and hollered, "Let er go!" We did, and the plow blade dropped into the ground.

"How long do you have to plow?" I asked when we were back on the tractor.

"I guess we can quit in an hour or so," Terry said. "Arvid will be ticked off if I don't finish today, but I want to play some ball. How's your new bow and arrow working? Have you shot any gophers yet?"

"Naw. Came close a couple of times, but they always see the arrow coming and duck."

Suddenly the plow reared up from the ground, looking like a wild mustang pawing at the air. The tractor lurched, and then the motor died.

We got off to look things over. I pretended I knew what I was looking for.

"The darn thing hit that rock," Terry said as he went back and toed it with his boot. "Look at the size of it! How in the heck did it get here? We've plowed this field for years and never hit it." For a minute he looked at it with a scowl. "Now I've got to reset the plow. Help me pull this lever down and lock it."

Our total weight added together didn't make two hundred pounds, and we couldn't quite get the lever depressed enough to catch the lock. Terry was a lot stronger than I was, but even he reached the point where he knew it was hopeless.

He sat down on the plow. "Why does it always happen to me?" he asked. His voice was quiet, defeated.

Chapter Sixteen

I once heard a child psychologist say that children learn to work not by being made to work, but by watching their parents work.

"Get your boots on," Dad instructed me. I was about five then, and we still had our wood cook stove. "Be sure to lace them up tight. I need your help cutting wood."

The left side of the stove had a narrow firebox covered by a cast-iron top that held the tea kettle, an ever present coffee pot, and our iron skillet. That was where Mom fried eggs over easy, crisped bacon, and sautéed vegetables.

The other side of the stove, the larger side, held the oven. A lever controlled the heat flow: push it in, and the heat was confined to the left side, but pull it out and the heat could flow around the oven so breads and cakes and pies could be baked. Neither side of the stove worked unless its glowing maw was fed a constant meal of wood pieces.

"Mom's almost out of wood," Dad explained as we traipsed outside. "If we don't get a few armloads up right away, we won't have any supper, or breakfast either."

I chased behind him in the snow, trying to keep up. "Hurry up now, and be sure to put your ear flaps down," Dad warned, glancing back to make sure I had listened. "You don't want to freeze your ears. Got your choppers?"

He picked up his Swede saw, a bow of metal four feet long with a coarse-toothed blade, and we headed to the slab pile. Slabs are the portion of a log with bark on it that is removed by sawmills when the log is squared up. He lifted a slab and put it in the saw buck so it was secured at waist height.

Dad sawed with a rhythm as he pushed and then pulled the blade across the wood. Spurts of sawdust spilled from the front of the cut and cascaded to the ground with each forward stroke. My job, Dad told me, was to catch each firewood-size piece as it was sawed off and add it to the growing stack of wood on the ground.

"Don't lift the wood or it'll pinch the saw blade," Dad warned. "Let it sag as I cut. When it begins to fall, catch it." He had me toss the wood in a pile off to the side. "Now you're logging," he said, and I saw him smile at me. "Boy, Mom's going to be surprised how fast we're getting this done."

I remember how important I felt as I helped Dad. I positioned my leather boots under the falling sawdust so it accumulated on my insteps. Some of the sweet smelling stuff worked its way under the bootlaces and into the eyelets. It filled the creases around the boot's tongue and stuck to the stitching.

I held out my arms while Dad loaded me with three or four of the smaller pieces of wood. He took all the rest. Together, we walked to the back porch and dumped the wood in a neat pile where Mom could easily get to it.

In the kitchen, I pulled a stool next to Dad and unlaced my boots, allowing the accumulated sawdust to spill onto the floor, proof that I had been to the woodpile and had worked like Dad.

Most of the year, Dad was an open pit miner, but in those days, equipment and technology were not available to dig the frozen ore out of the ground in winter. The ore would freeze to the gondola cars in which it was hauled, so the cars couldn't be dumped at the docks. Also, virtually all of the ore was shipped by rail to either Duluth or Two Harbors and then loaded into ships that made their way through the chain of Great Lakes to the steel mills out east. In the winter, the ports were ice-choked, and the Soo Locks at Sault Sainte Marie were frozen tight. Shipping was impossible. Most of the miners were laid off each winter, and those in Blackberry survived the lean times either with a family farm or working in the woods. Dad logged.

I idolized him. When Dad came home from the woods, he had pine pitch on his clothing. That was like high priced perfume to me. The wool socks drying in front of our space heater somehow gave me a sense that all was right in the world. I wanted to follow Dad wherever he went, and for the most part, I did.

When I was five, one of my uncles gave me a Boy Scout hatchet, and I was allowed to use it anytime I wanted, unsupervised. I set out to clear our twenty acres of all saplings and small trees.

"How would you like to come in the woods with me to-morrow?" Dad surprised me with that question one evening. "Don's not going to be with me," he said, referring to his logging partner. "He has to cut up a load of firewood for Old Man Bengston. I could use your help."

"Really? Can I take my hatchet with, and can I bring my own lunch?" I asked in disbelief. "What can I do out there? You know I can't cut with the Swede saw very good. What time will we leave? Do I get to stay all day?"

That night, I went to sleep hearing the sound of "Timber!" in my dreams.

In the morning, Mom fried eggs and bacon and mixed up pancakes for our breakfast. She made syrup to put on the hot cakes by adding brown sugar to boiling water, enough to form a sweet mixture that soaked into the cakes. We gobbled the food down in a hurry. Dad loaded his Swede saw, his axe, the lunches Mom had packed, and my hatchet into the car and drove to the "stumpage," acreage owned by Itasca County and from which Dad had purchased timber-cutting rights.

The sun rises late in northern Minnesota during the winter, and we arrived at the log landing just as the woods were getting light.

"Stand over there until I get this tree down," Dad ordered me. "I don't want it going the wrong way and hitting you."

He trimmed the lower branches from a balsam that was ten inches around. Then, just above the ground, he cut a notch in the tree with four sure strokes of his axe. With a few fluid sweeps of the saw, the tree started to shiver, then slowly topple. He didn't yell "Timber!" like I thought he would, and in the stillness of the morning, the only sound was the whisper of the evergreen as it fell into the fluffy snow on the ground.

"Now I'm ready for you, Dennis," Dad said. "You get to work with your hatchet and cut off all these limbs. I'll be back to check on you. Don't come over where I'm cutting. I can't be looking out for you all the time."

Dad left to do his work, and I started hacking away.

Balsam fir provides good pulp fiber for the paper making industry, but it used to be difficult for loggers to process. The trunk of each tree is covered with whorl after whorl of branches that have to be removed, trimmed closely to the tree trunk. Modern day logging has solved the problem with mechanized wood processors, but in 1948, the only way to remove the branches was with an axe. Adults could use the double-bit variety. Dad preferred a model called a cruiser's axe. It was lighter with a shorter handle than others, which made it easier to use. I had my hatchet.

I worked all morning, chipping away and severing the branches with my Lilliputian tool. By lunch time, I had accomplished my task: one naked tree, ready to be cut into four 100 inch logs, the standard measure of pulpwood.

The sound of Dad's saw and axe ceased, and he popped out from under a low hanging branch, taking me by surprise. "Let's go build a fire and heat up our lunch. Do you want a cup of coffee? I guess since you did a man's job this morning, you can have a man's drink."

As I watched the fire Dad built melt away snow from around its perimeter, I savored my bologna sandwich, took three of Mom's homemade oatmeal cookies, and dunked them in my half cup of hot coffee.

"Well, son, we've got more work to do," Dad said after a short rest. "What do you say? Are you up to one more tree?"

I was tired and a little cold, but I wasn't going to admit it. Dad had cut and limbed twenty trees to my one already. The work was physically demanding, even for someone as strong as Dad. After bringing a tree down, it had to have all its limbs chopped off. Then the tree was cut into eight-foot four-inch sections, and they needed to be stacked in piles. These piles of wood were placed alongside a skid road, a trail the logger cleared by hand. The skid road was wide enough for a horse and driver to maneuver a dray when the logs were skidded, or pulled, out of the woods to a landing or staging area.

Dad dropped another tree, sending a cloud of flakes floating in the air. This time I knew the drill, and as evening light changed the forest to shades of black and gray, I had another tree limbed. I was bushed. We packed up our tools, my hatchet and Dad's handsaw and axe, and we returned to the car in the deepening evening dusk.

At home, supper was on the table, and we peeled off our sweat-soaked clothes. We washed up in the basin by the sink and sat down to fill our bellies to bursting with one of Mom's hot-dishes. Fresh air and exercise combined to make my appetite voracious.

Even so, I was asleep almost before the meal was over. I think Dad was, too.

Chapter Seventeen

Dad's logging was done in the days before machines were used in the woods. The grapple loader hadn't been dreamed up, and someone had just thought of connecting a chain with sharp teeth to a gas engine. These early chainsaws were cumbersome, undependable, and expensive. No one in Blackberry owned one. Mechanized skidders were not even on the horizon. Everything was done with sheer muscle force.

Dad came home exhausted each night.

"Boy, Gen, I had a heck of a day," he'd say. "Cut 120 sticks today. The spruce was so thick it didn't have any limbs until the top two. Made pretty good money, with five sticks to the tree." A stick was the logger's term for a log.

"That's nice," Mom said. "Eat your spaghetti so I can finish the dishes."

"Don and I decided to skid tomorrow," Dad said between mouthfuls. "It's supposed to be cold again, and the dray should run on the pack pretty good. Make it a lot easier on the horse."

"Good. I've got to try to sew Janice's dress tomorrow, and my machine isn't stitching right. Could you take a look at it before you go to bed?"

"I kind of like skidding days. It feels good to see everything out at the landing in one pile. In a week, we should be paid by the mill. Maybe we can take in a movie then."

"By the way, Dennis needs a new pair of boots. His are getting tight."

"I suppose we'll be hauling on Thursday and Friday. Hope we get a good scale at the mill."

And so the non-conversation went on between my parents. It lasted for fifty years.

I know Dad found fulfillment in the woods. He was good at what he did and could cut about two cords of wood a day with his Swede saw. By the end of a week, he had twenty or so half-cord piles of logs neatly stacked along the makeshift skid road.

He and his partner Don would load them onto a dray and, with a horse's help, skid the logs to the main landing. There they hand-loaded each log onto a two-ton truck and hauled the load to the Blandin Paper Mill in Grand Rapids.

Loading was hard work. One man stood on the load on the truck, a pick in his hand. The pick was a tool with an axe-like handle, but the head was a wicked looking slim piece of steel that curved like a six-inch eagle's beak. It was swung like an axe into a log, where it stuck. Then the log could be pulled along.

"I'll work the load if you want the pile, Don. I don't mind." With that, Dad would climb onto the truck.

His partner upended a log from the pile, and just as it reached vertical, Dad swung the pick, burying it in the side of the log. Dad pulled up on the log, and Don lifted at the same time, his fingers under the down end. The log jumped onto the truck bed. Loaded to the hilt, the truck carried three cords of wood, 180 sticks, which meant this process had to be repeated 180 times. They made three trips a day to the mill, and by dark, they had money in their pockets.

Logging had many upsides. The woods were quiet in the winter with only the sounds of saws rasping their way through the timber. Deer would sometimes come to the cutting area, curious to see what was going on.

"I wish you could have been with me today, Dennis. A big buck and two does came so close to me I could see their eyelashes."

Then, too, the air was filled with the odor of Christmas every time a balsam fir came down. Jack pine gave off a distinct turpentine smell, and red pine produced a pitchy aroma. Aspen sawdust was pleasantly bitter when it was released by the saw blade, and spruce trees just smelled like wood to me.

The woods could also be a very dangerous place. One day, I followed Dad to a spot within walking distance from our house where he had felled several aspen the day before but had run out of daylight before they could be limbed. He took one swing with his axe. Then he stopped. He heaved the axe to his shoulder.

"Well, let's go home," he said in a calm voice.

I looked at him in puzzlement. "But we just got here. Why are we going home?"

With absolutely no emotion, he responded: "I cut my foot."

I thought he was joking. "You didn't really cut your foot, did you?"

"Yes, I cut my foot." We walked home then with the conversation running back and forth.

"You didn't really cut your foot."

"Yes, I really cut my foot."

By the time we arrived home, there was a distinct hint of pink left in the snow with each step Dad took. In the kitchen, Mom unlaced the boot on Dad's left foot while he was sitting on a kitchen chair. She gently pulled the boot off.

"Oh, Eddie, what did you do?" she gasped as she poured bright red blood from Dad's boot into a basin.

"I sharpened my axe last night, and the first swing I took, it went right through the popple limb," Dad said grimly. "The blade hit the crust on the snow and came back at me. Gen, is it bad?"

"It's bleeding so hard, I can't see, but I think you split your big toe," Mom answered. "I'll get it wrapped up and see if the bleeding slows down. I guess this means you won't be working for a while."

"Call Vic. See if he'll take me into town."

Dad was taken to the doctor with Mom's makeshift bandage holding his toe together and staunching the flow of blood. The doctor stitched him up. When he came home, he told Mom the doctor said to tell her she had done a fine job of bandaging the wound.

The toenail on his left foot bore the scar of that day for the rest of his life.

Chapter Eighteen

Dad was a good worker, and he was always looking for jobs he could take on to supplement his mining and logging earnings. Every August, in his spare time, he hired out to work on a threshing crew at a couple of local farms. As he often did, Dad took me along.

I was standing next to a tin monster that had two spouts coming from one end and a heavy tongue for towing on the other. It seemed to be a sheet-metal box. I watched, rapt, as our neighbor Vic pulled an old tractor up about twenty feet in front of the contraption. He and two other men lifted a long, heavy drive-belt, put one end around a pulley on the side of the tractor, and did the same on the sheet-metal box.

Then Vic pulled a lever on the tractor, putting it into gear, and the monster came alive. It started rattling and banging with such a din that I jumped back a few steps. The men who were standing around started to laugh. Dad put his hand on my shoulder. "Why don't you come with me? I'm loading wagons in the field. It'll be safer and quieter out there."

I wanted to get away from the din, so we set off walking.

"You remember this don't you?" Dad asked. "We were in the next field over last week when we shocked oats."

Of course I remembered. On a late August day, I had been at this farm with Dad when he tried to teach me how to build a shock. Vic had been pulling a reaper. The machine would cut the grain and then, by some sort of mechanical magic, would tie the shafts into bundles. These bound sheaves were kicked out to the side every few feet, leaving a trail of them behind.

"We're going to shock these," Dad had said. "Take two of them like this and lean them against each other." He stood them together, grain end up. "Now two more, and then two more." I watched as Dad built what looked to be a miniature pup tent with the six sheaves. Then he leaned two more, one against each end, and finally, he laid one across the top. "That'll keep them dry if it rains," he declared, and he moved on to build another shock.

I tried, but right away I ran into trouble. I could only carry one bundle at a time, and when I got two together and propped them up, they slid to the ground like they were too tired to stand. Finally, when I'd trained them to stay, I dragged in two more. I leaned them against what was now standing and watched in dismay as the whole structure toppled to the ground. After several minutes, I was still struggling, but Dad had twenty shocks up.

It didn't take much to distract me from my frustration. "Hey Dad, did you see that big gopher?" I asked excitedly. I sat motionless by the gopher's burrow, and a minute or two later, his head popped up. I froze—he froze, his beady eyes staring at me, unblinking. For several seconds we faced off, only feet apart. Finally, I twitched when a fly lit on my nose. Down his burrow the gopher went. We played that game for a long time, until the gopher got tired and didn't return to stare at me again.

The next week, Dad and I were in the field together again, along with two teams of horses hitched to hay wagons. Four tractors that were on hand also pulled a wagon. On either side of each wagon walked a man with a pitchfork, and as he came to a shock, he would pick up the sheaves with his fork and gently lay them on the wagon, one at a time so as not to jar the grain heads loose. I watched as Dad repeated this same motion over and over again.

I caught sight of a bit of gray fur in the stubble of the field. "Look at those mice run! Do you think they ever run up somebody's pant leg? I bet that would feel real funny. What do I do if one does run up my pant leg?"

I chased mice and asked questions. Dad just kept pitching bundles of oats.

"Hey Ed, this is the last load before lunch," Vic said. "Why don't you and Dennis go in and clean up."

On the way back to the farm house, Dad told me about the machine that had scared me. "That thing by the barn is a threshing machine. The belt you saw takes the power from the tractor. The tractor makes the belt move, and the belt makes the thresher work. I'll show you how it works once they shut it off."

When we got to the barn, the thresher was still hammering away. "Watch now, the guy on the load will feed the oat bundles into the hopper on top. There are beaters inside that knock the grain loose and the hulls off each oat," Dad continued while he pointed to the different parts. "Then a big fan inside blows the straw and chaff out. See it coming out of that chute?"

As we got ready for lunch, all of the men started taking off their shirts. So did I. Everybody headed to the watering tank. Most of the men submerged their whole torso in the water, coming up blowing and snorting like the horses that also drank there. Someone threw me a towel, and I joined the other "men" in drying off. We headed to a table made from two-inch planks set on top of sawhorses. Lunch was mashed potatoes and gravy, roast beef, bread, cooked vegetables, cheeses, fresh vegetables from the garden, pies of different sorts, and even a scoop of ice cream. I drank two glasses of lemonade, but the men who had been working all morning drank quarts of liquid to replace what they had sweated out.

Then it was back to the field. By the end of the day, every shock had been removed and fed to the tin monster, and Dad and I headed home, proud of our day's work.

Chapter Nineteen

Mom did her part to make ends meet as well.

"Eddie, I'm thinking about picking potatoes this fall," Mom said one morning. "I'd like to earn some extra Christmas money."

Dad looked shocked. "What are you talking about, Gen? Don't you realize how much work that is? You won't last one morning out there. You've already got enough to do around here."

Mom cleared the table and went to the sink, humming to herself. Dad thought that was the end of it.

Two days later, Mom was up at five-thirty, as usual. She fixed Dad's lunch pail and kissed him goodbye when he left for work. Then she put on her oldest pair of work pants, wrapped a blue bandana around her hair, and grabbed a pair of gloves. "Come on kids," she urged us. "You're going to play in Al Johnson's yard while I work in his potato field."

Blackberry was a great place to raise "spuds." The soil was sandy, which allowed for good drainage and prevented blight. That year had been a good year, and Al Johnson was expecting a bountiful crop. But he needed pickers, eight of them.

In the field, two workers were needed to load and unload hundred pound sacks of potatoes. The workers had to be able to pick up the heavy sacks, swing them up onto a wagon bed, and take them to the root cellar. There, they had to unload the bags and carry them down a short flight of stairs. No way could Mom do that.

"Gen, you can work on the viner," Al said. "Just be careful that you don't lean too far over and get caught in the conveyor. Mildred will be working beside you, and she'll tell you what to do."

Al owned the only potato viner in Blackberry, as well as a mechanical potato digger. He had his tractor already hooked up to the digger, and the digger was hooked to the viner. Five workers set off for the field, two standing on the running boards on each side, and one on the back of the viner.

Janice and I were left to amuse ourselves in the yard. We played with a litter of kittens. When we tired of that, we stood near the fence and watched the cows watch us, and then we explored the inside of the empty barn. Eventually, we wandered back to where Mom was working.

The tractor stopped at the edge of the field, and Al got off and lowered the digging blade. The blade was like a three-foot wide shovel that tilted into the ground, perhaps sixteen inches under the soil. The whole mess: vines, potatoes, and dirt, were pushed up onto a vibrating chain-link conveyor which shook most of the dirt free.

Mildred leaned over close to Mom's ear. "The potatoes and vines will drop onto the conveyor of the viner," she yelled above the racket. "It's our job to get the vines off, pick out any rocks, and grab any rotten potatoes that go by. It works best to roll the vines into a ball and then throw them over the side."

All morning long Mom worked on that noisy, vibrating contraption. She banged her knee on the steel frame of the viner when it hit a rut and lurched sideways. Her back ached from hunching over the conveyor, and her fingers were bruised and swollen.

"Gen, you were quite a trooper out there this morning," Al complimented as they headed to lunch.

"Thanks," Mom smiled.

Mom, Janice, and I brought our lunch over to a birch tree and sat in the shade while we ate. Mom took her bandana off and wiped the sweat from her face. This left it streaked from the dust that had mixed with her sweat and turned to mud. She didn't mind; she had made two dollars.

After we ate, Mom went back out and picked all afternoon. Still, she made it home in time to clean up, and she had supper ready when Dad walked in the door.

"I worked for Al today," Mom announced over dinner. "We picked the forty acres across the road. Only had two breakdowns, but the guys fixed the conveyor both times."

"You picked potatoes?" Dad said, surprised. "Are you okay? Didn't hurt anything?"

"No, I'm fine," Mom assured him.

"Good," Dad said. There was a note of approval in his voice that faded as quickly as it came. "Pass the roast."

After that, Mom followed the picker from farm to farm, and she developed some good friendships with a couple of other women who were pickers. The last farm she worked at that first year was owned by two brothers and a sister. The brothers were quite outgoing people, but the sister, Gertrude, was not. Janice and I had to stay with Gertrude while Mom picked.

"You can play outside, but don't go any further than the edge of the grass," Mom commanded before she left. "Stay away from that dog. It's a German shepherd and they say he was a war dog," she warned. "He bites."

When Janice and I went into the kitchen, Gertrude turned and stared at us. She never said a word, just stared. Then she went back to working at her stove.

Gertrude's legs were swollen and black, and knotted varicose veins stood out like blue-black lumps. For some reason, Gertrude had wrapped strips of dirty cloth around her calves, and the bandages sagged. In places where the rags had come undone, her skin was visible. She looked like a horror picture of a mummy come to life. From time to time Gertrude would turn and stare at us as we sat at the kitchen table, but she never did speak. Eventually, Janice and I thought a biting dog would make better company, and we went outside.

After the picking season ended, Mom went back to being Mom, and her career was put on hold until next year.

It was about a week later, just at dusk, when rows of flames roared across Al's field. I stood in our yard and watched the fire. "Al's burning the potato vines," I called into the house. "I saw him raking them up this morning. Let's go over and see."

Mom, Dad, Janice, and I walked across Al's field. It was dark by then, and a harvest moon had risen above. Rows of flames danced across the field, and smoke wafted our way. Al and his wife and their two sons were making sure the fire didn't jump to any dry grass near the edge of the field.

"Hey Gen," called Al. "There go all of the vines you threw off. Doesn't the smoke smell great? Fall is in the air."

I could also smell baked potatoes.

"Dennis, come here," Al's oldest son, Jim, called to me. "Dig down with the toe of your boot. There, see it. It's a potato, baked right in the ground. The digger missed a few."

It was Bill, Jim's younger brother, who fired the first shot. He hit Jim in the back with a potato, and a food fight broke out. Most of the potatoes were so hot it was impossible to hold them long. In one motion, Jim scooped up a potato from the ground and, like a shortstop making a fielding play, fired it back at Bill. If they were well cooked, the potatoes splattered when they hit, turning to mashed potatoes. The partially cooked missiles impacted with a thud. But it was getting cold in the October evening. Too soon it was time to go home to bed.

We had a great Christmas that year. With her potato picking money, Mom bought Dad the set of car-top boat carriers he wanted.

"What the hell did you do that for?" he said. But he was smiling.

Chapter Twenty

Even when I was little, I was expected to do what I could to help out. That was especially true when it came to gardening and picking wild berries.

Each night, Dad gave his blueberry report. He'd hunted the land in Blackberry for years, and he knew most of the bogs and ridges where the best berries grew. Starting in late July, he began scouting the patches. One evening he came home with a big grin.

"They're hanging like grapes the size of your fingernail. Can you believe this?" He had ripped a couple of bushes out of the ground, and he lifted them for us to see. Blueberries hung in clusters. "The ground is blue," he said with excitement. "And they're right down by a bog where it will be nice and cool picking."

Mom plucked a few off Dad's pilfered bushes and popped them in her mouth. "Mmm, these are good," she said, licking her lips.

"Really juicy and sweet. I better call a few of the ladies and go picking tomorrow."

The "ladies" consisted of my aunt Genevieve, Mildred, and Mae. "Eddie just got back from the woods with the best blueberries you've ever seen," she told them on the phone.

Mom scrambled to fix lunch for three that evening, then washed the smaller round bathtub clean. She found her coffee can bucket with the wire handle and, along with two smaller cans, she placed them in the tub. We were ready to go.

The next morning everyone gathered at our house. Mom didn't drive, had never learned, but the other ladies did. Dad led the way to the woods. A short walk over a jack pine ridge and we were there. The ground was covered with blueberry bushes laden with fruit. When Dad left for work, four women and five kids started to pick.

"Mom, did you bring my sweatshirt?" I called.

"Just wait a little while. Once the sun gets higher, it's going to heat up in a hurry, and you'll be taking it off again." She handed me my bucket. "Don't eat too many. We've got to fill the tub by dinner-time."

On my knees, I started to pick, and I filled my pint can in no time. "Hey Mom, I'm full over here. Where's the tub?"

"Under the white pine on the ridge. Are you picking clean? You know I want them picked clean."

"Yeah, they are," I lied. Picking clean meant going slower and not stripping the berries off the branches, leaves and all. It meant being more discriminate, taking only the ripe berries, and leaving the green on the bushes. It also meant that when we got home, there was less work to do because the gallons of berries were easier to prepare for canning.

"Janice? Where are you?"

"Over here, Mom," she answered.

Janice's blond hair was shiny clean and pulled back in two ponytails. She wore a bright colored shirt so she could be easily spotted; a four-year-old can disappear from sight in the brush too quickly. Her fair skinned cheeks were red from the sun, but she was smiling her usual impish smile.

"Is your cup full? If it is, bring it here and dump it in my container." Janice gave Mom her cup and ran for the lemonade jug.

"Janice Herschbach, you get back here right now!" Mom suddenly hollered as she dumped the cup's contents. "You filled your blueberry cup with moss and then sprinkled a few berries on top. Empty that out right now, and fill it with blueberries. Don't do that again."

Janice was busted.

I moved from bush to bush, looking for those that grew in the shade of large rocks or old pine stumps. There I could find the really big clusters of berries, and the berries themselves were juicier. I picked a quart in one place without having to move.

By mid-morning, the sun was higher in the sky like Mom had promised, and the flies came out. "Oow, Mom I just got nailed by a horsefly!" I cried, slapping my shoulder. "Geez, I hate them. Where's the bug dope?"

Insect repellents were not well developed in those days. All we had was an oily stuff that came in a small glass bottle. We'd smear it on, but it seemed like it only attracted more flies.

"Dennis, you know I don't want you saying 'geez.' Quit complaining and fill your can one more time before lunch."

By mid-day, I'd hear, "Dennis, stop eating those berries and put them in your can. Stop goofing around or your father will hear about this."

But there were toads to find in the shade, and meadow voles dashed past my feet, running for safety. I found a skeleton of some long dead animal, and I tried to put it together to see if I could identify it. Then I lay on my back in the shade of a pine, looking at the sky that was as blue as wild aster blossoms. I'd watch the small, cottony clouds drift by and think of what it must be like to fly like a bird. In the heat of the day, the aroma of jack pine sap mixed with the smell of sweet fern. If I close my eyes on a hot day, I can still smell that.

"My back is killing me, but just look," Mom boasted late in the afternoon. "I think this is the first time I've filled the tub in one day. Eddie is going to be so happy to see how much we picked. Gather up all your stuff, kids. Dennis, do you have your shirt? It was hanging on a branch down by the bog the last time I saw it."

Every summer, we tried to put up at least fifty quarts of blueberries.

"Eddie, I think we picked almost a year's worth today," Mom said when we got home. "Just look at these, and look how clean they are. Picking was so easy."

Then she got out a larger tub, filled it half full with cold water, and dumped in a few quarts of berries. All of the pieces of sticks and leaves floated to the surface, along with a few bugs. These could be skimmed off. This process went on until all of the berries had been cleaned and washed. When our day's loot was ready to preserve the next morning, Mom could sit down for a few minutes before bed.

Not all of the berries made it to the fruit jars. Nothing can top fresh blueberry pie or a bowl full of sugared berries with ice cold milk.

Chapter Twenty-One

In the late 1920s, at the beginning of the Great Depression, Dad's father had owned a fairly large farm by the Mississippi, in Blackberry. Dad told me that he remembered when his family was short of money and had to sell their first cow. Eventually, another cow went, and then another. This continued for several months until they had no more cows.

Then they had to sell both teams of horses. Finally, all they owned was the empty farm, and eventually, that was taken too.

Before 1929, my grandfather had been a respected person in Blackberry. He had served as the chairman of the township board and as the town constable. After his family lost everything in the depression, he dropped from sight, and he and his family moved from shack to shack, trying to eke out a living.

Dad's whole family had to work at whatever they could find just to survive. More than once, Dad recollected picking blueberries to sell in town for ten cents a quart. He helped his father cut stove wood for town people. Sometimes they used a "long axe," the colloquial term for cutting wood on state property to which they had no cutting rights. They lived on rabbits and deer shot out of season. The whole family was expected to help in their extensive garden. Work was picked up piecemeal wherever it could be found. My father was scared by his childhood misfortune, and his fear came out in the way we lived while I was growing up.

"Eddie, we need a new sofa," Mom complained. "The stuffing is spilling out of this one, and the springs are poking through the back."

"For crying out loud!" Dad exploded. "I get laid off every winter, and we can hardly make it when I'm logging. What if I got hurt in the woods again? Then who'd pay the bills?"

"It's no wonder we don't have anything. Name one person on this road who doesn't have more than we do. Do you think everything they have is paid for?" Mom was exasperated.

"That's their problem. We'll get a sofa when we can pay for it straight out."

That's the way Dad operated, cash on the barrelhead. Some wounds of childhood never heal.

Mom's family had weathered the depression fairly well, even though her Pa had been a miner, too. She and Dad were from two different cultures, and one or the other was not going to be happy.

Since Mom had never learned to drive, Dad had to take her everywhere.

"Eddie, I need to go into town this afternoon. We need a few things from the grocery store."

"We were just there three days ago," Dad complained. "Why didn't you get them then?"

"I didn't need them then. You expect me to keep track of everything around here, don't you? I'm sick and tired of being stuck out here day after day. You get to go to work and be with other people. What do I have?"

"Yeah, that's right. I go have fun at work." Dad's voice was on edge.

"Listen mister, I work every bit as hard as you do—and longer hours too. Don't you forget it."

"Fine, grab your purse. We'll go if you stop complaining."

Mom folded her arms across her chest. "I don't want to go if you're going to be that way. I have to beg for everything around here. Go read your sports page. It doesn't matter."

"Let's go, I said."

Dad headed outside, and Mom went to the sink to do the dishes, humming a random tune as she always did when she wanted to irritate Dad. Eventually she'd put on her lipstick and comb her hair, step outside and call to Dad. "Eddie, I'm ready to go."

We'd all pile into the car and drive to Grand Rapids in frigid silence. Once there, Mom always hurried through her errands, rushing from store to store, buying what few things she could with her limited funds. Dad sat in the car the whole time and complained about what was taking her so long.

Because she didn't drive, Mom was continually stranded in the backwoods of Blackberry. Once in a while she would walk to her nearest friend's house, but Mae lived over a mile away, down a road that was gravel and perpetually dusty. The only real variety in Mom's life was that each new season brought with it a different kind of work required to keep the household going.

Canning season started at the end of June and ran until nearly September. We had a huge garden that was large enough to raise all of the vegetables for our family for the coming year, and everything had to be canned.

Before it could be set away, the crop had to be grown.

"Dennis, I want you to pick potato bugs tomorrow," Dad ordered me. "Gen, did you hear that? Make sure he picks the bugs before he goes off into the woods. Let's make a deal, son. I'll give you a penny for every ten bugs you have at the end of the day."

The next morning, I wasn't out of bed before I heard Mom call, "Don't run off today, Dennis. You have to pick potato bugs. Eat your breakfast and get started."

I took an old jelly jar with a lid on it and headed for the acre-sized patch. "There you are, you little bugger. You can't get away that easy," I muttered as I picked the yellow and black striped beetles from the potato leaves. Each plant had to be thoroughly examined; leaves had to be turned upside down and scrutinized for the beetles whose larvae could eat holes in the vegetation. When Dad got home from work, I presented him with the smelly mess of dead beetles roasted in the sun, and I collected my four cents.

That night at the supper table, Dad said, "Dennis, the strawberries need weeding. Gen, did you hear that? Make sure he weeds the strawberries tomorrow before he runs off." And the following day, I weeded the strawberries, grasping the weeds by their green throats and ripping them out of the ground.

Next I heard, "Dennis, the beans need to be hoed. Gen, make sure he hoes the beans tomorrow."

I hated the hoe, a big heavy one that had once been used to mix cement. It hadn't been cleaned well, and the dried cement on its blade and handle doubled its weight. My arms soon tired, and then my half-hearted whacks became misdirected, wiping out bean plants as I went down the row.

Mom came out to look at what I was doing. "Why don't you use the cultivator?" she suggested. "Maybe that would work better."

I went behind the garage and pulled out the archaic thing. It had one two-foot wheel in front; attached to the wheel was a pair of handles similar to those of a wheelbarrow, but higher off the ground, about chest high on me. The undercarriage held three curved tines that dug into the soil. I positioned it next to the plants in the first row of the garden and let the tines penetrate the soil. Then I leaned into the handles and pushed as hard as I could. I moved down the row with the cultivator's three steel fingers clawing the soil and tearing up the weeds. I had to rest for a few minutes before turning around and heading back up the row. It was only dire threats of what would happen "when your father gets home" that kept me focused on the job.

By the end of June, the green beans and peas were ready for harvest, and the canning season moved ahead full bore.

"The forecast is for hot weather tomorrow, in the low nineties. It's always hot when I plan to run the pressure cooker," Mom groaned. Nevertheless, she took out her cooker, along with the quart canning jars with their *Ball* label etched on the side. All three of us, Mom, Janice, and I, headed down to the garden.

"Be sure to hold the vine with one hand and pick the bean off with your other," Mom directed. "We don't want to pull any plants out or break off beans that aren't ready. No, that one's too small, Janice. See, about this size."

It took only a half hour to pick the beans. We carried them up to the house, washed them, and started snapping. Each bean was broken into about three pieces, just bite size.

Mom sent us out to play while she scalded the jars, along with their lids and the screw-on rings. Then she packed the beans into the jars and stood four full jars in the pressure cooker. The cooker lid was equipped with an escape valve, an opening on which rested an aluminum weight. Once the water inside the cooker began to vigorously boil, the weight danced a jig on top of the kettle, settling into a staccato rhythm. With the heat from the stove and the steam released from the valve, the kitchen was transformed into a veritable a Finnish bathhouse.

Mom had a healthy fear of her pressure cooker. If Janice and I came back inside too soon, she would shoo us away. "Stay back now! I'm going to open the cooker. Sometimes the lid blows off these things and people get hurt."

She'd take out the hot jars of canned beans and set them on the counter. Then she would start the process all over again. Her hair would soak up the beads of sweat on her forehead and mat together, and her blouse would stick to her skin. Sometime in the afternoon, in between batches, she cooked the evening meal.

Mom lined the jars up on the counter, and we'd wait for their telltale "pop" to sound. No pop, no seal, and the jar had to be processed again.

"Dennis, keep your fingers off those jars," Mom commanded. "If you touch those lids before they pop on their own, I'll have to do the whole batch over again. Get out of here, NOW!"

The beans were only the beginning. Peaches, pears, cherries, and plums came off railroad cars packed in wooden lugs, and all of it had to be put up for the winter. During the season, different berries ripened at intervals: strawberries came first, then raspberries and blackberries, and finally chokecherries in mid-August. At home, Mom would mash them into a pulp. She cooked the pulp down, added pectin and sugar, and poured the hot mixture into jars.

As the jelly was cooking, Mom melted paraffin wax in a small pot, and while I watched, I'd chew a piece of the wax until my jaw muscles cramped. Mom poured the melted wax on top of the preserves in the jar, and it hardened there, forming an airtight seal that had to be loosened and lifted off when the jar's contents were to be eaten. Usually it broke into several pieces so that the first few servings had chunks of paraffin mixed in.

By the end of summer, the shelves in our basement looked like a grocery store with rows and rows of canned fruits, jams, jellies, and garden vegetables.

On a cold winter day, there was absolutely nothing better than sitting down to a bowl of blueberry sauce along with a piece of Mom's warm, homemade bread spread with real butter. Nothing could compare, unless, of course, the bowl was filled with canned cherries. I know the Good Book says not to lay up your treasures on earth, but we sure felt secure once the year's supply of food was "put away."

Chapter Twenty-Two

Not everyone in Blackberry toiled at making a living. There was one man who lived an ascetic life. Emil lived off the land, heated his hovel with wood, and shunned civilization. He terrified me.

I was five years old and standing in the Blackberry Store when a giant ragged man walked through the door. His gray beard hung in knots around his face, whiskers long, misshapen, and scraggly. He was dressed in rags and wore, low rubber boots held on by pieces of rope. I could only cower behind Dad's legs as I looked up at Emil, a genuine hermit who had walked the three miles from his shelter in the woods by the river. He had come into civilization to buy staples, and because he spoke little English, he communicated his needs mostly with motions and grunts. Emil didn't buy much: some salt and sugar, coffee, a small bag of flour, bacon, a few eggs, and two cans of beans. He paid for his cache, slung his gunnysack over his shoulder, and with his shuffling gait, he began to walk home.

No one talked to him, and most did their business in a hurry and left the store quickly. Emil was most unsavory, both in appearance and in the way he smelled. His eyes glowered from beneath heavy, untrimmed eyebrows, and his long gray hair made a good effort of escaping from under his worn hat. Few people associated with Emil. Once in a while, an older Finn who spoke the language would stop by to speak Finnish with him, but mostly he was a recluse. Dad said he had been deer hunting near Emil's shack one fall and had heard someone talking rather excitedly. Eventually, he found Emil carrying on an animated conversation with a tree.

I sometimes wondered what else Emil did by himself. Did he stay up all night reading books by candlelight? Did he sit and think, or maybe carve? My boyhood curiosity was never satisfied.

Periodically, Emil would walk past our house. When I saw him coming, I would run and hide. He would shuffle by, his torn rubber boots held on by their ropes and his burlap bag slung over his hunched shoulder. He stared at the ground, oblivious to what was ahead.

Emil died when I was eight, and I was surprised to find I rather missed seeing him coming down the road. I don't know how he died. He may have had a heart attack or even cancer. He was so withdrawn, I doubt if he would have complained to anyone if he had problems. One of the few people who visited him found him dead in his bed one winter day. Neighbors said that he had shoes and suits of clothes stored in his cabin that had never been worn. There was a rumor that he had money he never spent on himself.

One day, several months after Emil died, I was walking with Dad down on the river bottoms near what had been Emil's home. For the first time, I saw his ramshackle cabin.

"That's all that's left of what Emil had," Dad said. "He lived a pretty sad life."

The place was a tar-paper shack with a couple of small, square windows. I don't think enough light could have entered for him to read a newspaper; trees grew right up to the walls and shaded everything. The windows were high enough off the ground that when I stood on tiptoes and tried to look in, I couldn't see over the window sill. That was probably just as well. Emil had been so private in life that he might as well remain anonymous in death.

Dad and I turned away and followed Emil's walking path down to the river. As we neared the water, I saw a cup hanging from a branch. A spring bubbled out of the river bank beneath it, a slow trickle that oozed from the sandy bank and collected in a small pool Emil had hollowed out of the soil. Here was Emil's water source. Suddenly, so near his haunts, Emil's lifestyle became extremely attractive to me. I wanted nothing more than to live in a wilderness retreat and drink water from a spring, scooped up in a cup that had been left hanging on an overhead branch.

It wasn't the first time I'd felt that way. When I was six, reading material was in rather short supply in my house. I read and re-read an adult Zane Grey novel we had about a handsome and strong young man who chose to live far from civilization in a cave in the forest. The cave itself fascinated me. It had a fireplace, warm animal skins draped the walls, and it was filled with the wonderful aroma of venison cooking on an open fire.

This was the life I wanted to live. I wanted to be free to roam woodland trails. I wanted to hunt and fish and trap, unfettered by the presence of people. However, the first time I read the book to the end, I was crushed when the hero suffered a most unfortunate and unexpected end. He met a woman, of all things, and she was a city woman. To me, a child who truly wanted to be a hermit, this was about the worst thing that could happen. It turned out the hero could not stand the loneliness of a solitary life after falling in love, and he gave up his cave to live with her. I read the book several times and each time wished I could rewrite the ending.

I would have had it end as Emil's life did. He never left his shack in the woods, and to my way of thinking, died happy.

Chapter Twenty-Three

Unfortunately, I couldn't follow the way of a hermit. I had to go to school. In Blackberry we had no kindergarten, and I entered first grade as a six-year-old.

"Hurry, come quickly," Mom had called to me throughout my toddler years. I'd run to the sofa that stood under the front room window. "There it is." She pointed at the long, yellow bus. "Next year you'll get to ride on it. See, it's stopping at the Johnsons' to pick up their kids. Won't that be exciting?"

Even though Mom tried to prepare me, the transition from my carefree days as a "preschooler" to being confined in a structured classroom was difficult for me. I was used to running wild in the woods all day, hacking trees and hunting both real and imaginary animals. That was taken from me the day I entered first grade. When it came time for me to board the bus on my first day, I climbed the stairs carrying my bag lunch and a bundle of misgivings.

Miss Warner, my first grade teacher, was waiting at the door of the school for the first graders and any new students in grades two and three. She ushered us into the classroom we all shared. I was forced to sit in a desk bolted to two long boards that resembled sleigh runners. The row of desks, all attached to these same two boards, looked like a sled that could slide down a winter hill—if we could only get the darn thing out of the room. I sat second from the back in the second row from the windows. My mind wandered to the woods, to the birch tree in our yard that I loved to sit beneath.

At about ten o'clock, I was bored and hungry. I raised my hand.

"Miss Warner. Can I go get a sandwich from my lunch?"

"No, we all eat together. For now you have to stay in your seat and finish the work I assigned to you." I was used to eating when I was hungry, going to the bathroom when I had to go, and getting a drink when I was thirsty. I could tell by a few snickers from the older students that I had made a serious faux pas.

Eventually, lunchtime came. "You have thirty minutes to go outside and play," Miss Warner told us. "There is to be no pushing or shoving. You can play kickball if you want, but make sure everyone gets a chance." We filed out of the lunchroom.

"Get out of my way!" one third grade boy said to another who happened to be standing where he wanted to be.

"Make me!" the other shot back.

"I can't make you! You're already made, and God did a pretty lousy job!"

The boy who had first thrown down the challenge advanced, his chest thrust forward, his jaw jutting out. The other held his ground. Both were farm boys who were used to hard work, and now they were prepared to square off.

"I said, get out of my way!" the first boy barked.

"And I said, make me!"

By this time they were toe to toe and face to face, sneering at each other. It was then that one, with a quick jab, shoved the other, and he retaliated by shoving back. They charged each other, grabbing and tackling until they went down in a heap of arms and legs, cursing. One got an arm free and hit the other on his nose; blood began to trickle down his upper lip. A shirt was ripped, a knee skinned. A crowd gathered to watch. "That a way, Jimmy! Hit him in the eye. Then he won't be able to see."

"Bill, use your knee, pin him down."

"Do you need help, Jim? I'll help if you want."

When the bell rang at the end of recess, everyone ran for the school. The two warriors, bloodied and bruised, finally broke off the battle and separated. Each wiped his nose, spit out blood, dusted off the dirt and loose grass, and tried to enter the classroom without drawing attention to himself.

"Jimmy, Bill, what was going on out there?"

"Nothing, Miss Warner," they mumbled.

"I wouldn't want to have to send a note to your parents on the very first day of school. Now take out your books and get busy."

"Yes, Miss Warner," they answered, a little more confidently.

When we were dismissed at the end of the day, I was anxious to know what was going to happen. But I saw Bill and Jimmy laughing and horsing around, friends once again. Evidently whatever had triggered the playground battle was long forgotten.

The bus delivered me home, and I ran into the house to tell Mom what I had done that day. "First we sang some songs, but I didn't know the words, so I kind of just moved my mouth. Then we recited the alphabet. You know some kids couldn't do it? We had lunch and played outside. Then we went inside some more."

I didn't mention the part about the fight on the playground.

Chapter Twenty-Four

I became somewhat accustomed to the rhythm of school. Monday morning: get dressed, eat breakfast, and get on the bus. Suffer through a day of confinement.

Tuesday through Thursday: follow the routine set by Monday.

Friday: awaken early to watch the clock all day long, counting the minutes until I would be freed.

Finally, school would be dismissed, and I could go home to shed my one good flannel shirt and my trousers that had been handed down from an older cousin. I put on a shirt with frayed cuff edges and a worn collar, pulled on holey pants, and headed for the woods.

One good thing did come of school; by early winter, I had learned to read. A new world of fantasy opened up to me.

"First graders, take out your book about the woodsman. That will be our lesson today. I want you to read silently while the second graders are working on their penmanship. I'll be with the third graders while they practice spelling."

I could hardly wait to take out the book. We had only gotten to the second page when we started it the day before. I wanted to take the thin and tattered book home, but Miss Warner said the books had to stay in school. I began reading from the beginning. I didn't want to miss a thing.

There was once an old man who lived deep in the woods.

He had enough food for breakfast.

He sat down and prayed for help.

He ate his meal.

He went hunting.

From that point on, I was with the woodsman every step of the way. The old man and I spotted a flock of ducks, sprinkled a few grains of corn on the ground, and then suspended our net over the area. When ducks came for the corn, the net dropped. We had food. As we walked down the trail, we found a buck tangled in a thicket. The woodsman shot the deer with his rifle, and we started to drag it home. Before we went far, we found a spot in the river where fish were trapped in a pool. Naturally, we netted them out. The woodsman and I made it home to our cozy log cabin carrying enough food for many days. God had provided.

"Dennis, I said put the woodsman book in your desk. Everyone else is ready to begin reviewing addition tables, and you're still reading. Pay attention now." Everyone giggled, not just the older kids this time, and my face turned red.

The long awaited Christmas vacation finally arrived, and I went to visit my grandparents, my mother's parents, in Keewatin. They lived only a half block from the main railroad line that came out of the iron ore pits. In 1949, the mining industry didn't have the behemoth trucks now used to haul ore. Instead, the ore was hauled from the bottoms of open pit mines by coal-fired steam locomotives. The fireboxes of the huge engines were hand fired, and the fireman, who shoveled coal into the gaping opening of the engine's furnace, had to strain his back to stoke a hot fire as the engineer "poured the steam" to the massive pistons that drove the wheels.

There was a pattern of sounds that I found strangely comforting. It began with a measured PHWOOSH...PHWOOSH... PHWOOSH...PHWOOSH as giant cylinders powered by steam pushed the rods that made the wheels turn. During my first Christmas vacation from school, I fell asleep at my grandparents' house to that familiar rhythm.

My grandmother woke me the next morning. "I'm afraid something really bad happened last night," she told me in a serious voice. "Your school burned down. There's nothing left of it."

While I had slept, the archaic coal furnace in Blackberry Elementary had overheated, causing a fire to break out in the two-story wooden building. In a matter of minutes, the school was engulfed in flames. Blackberry did not even have a volunteer fire department. Not only that, there were no hydrants to which they could attach fire hoses. There wasn't even a nearby lake or pond to pump water from. The school burned completely to the ground before the fire trucks from Grand Rapids could make the twenty minute run. By daybreak, all that remained were a few smoldering timbers, some twisted steel rods, and a heap of tin from furnace.

I had questions.

"Did my desk get burned up?"

"Yes, everything was burned."

"Did they save our books?" I immediately thought of my favorite woodsman story.

"I don't know. I doubt they could save much."

"Where will I go to school?"

"It's too soon to know that."

Two weeks later, Dad attended a special school board meeting and, as he did from most meetings, came home mad. "That damn Hantly says Blackberry isn't big enough for a school, that we don't have enough students to rebuild for. I stood up and told him what I thought, but he said the decision had already been made."

"Where will they bus the kids to?" Mom asked, concerned.

"Warba. They say there's plenty of room there. I asked Hantly if he'd like his kids riding a bus half the day, but he just sneered and said, 'I don't choose to live in the woods.' Some chairman he is."

On the first day back from Christmas vacation, all the Blackberry students met at the village hall. Miss Warner had us gather around, and she tried to dispel our fears and anxieties. "Each day your bus will pick you up and take you to Warba. You know your driver, Mr. Laine, and he will make sure you get safely to school."

We first graders sat frozen, eyes wide with disbelief.

"Your new school is much bigger than the one that burned down. It's so big that each grade has its very own classroom. But for the rest of this year, we will remain together, just like we have been."

I was one of the first students picked up on the morning route. The route was reversed in the afternoon, and I was one of the last to be dropped off. I hated that extra time on the bus. There were fights and bullying, complaints and coarse talk. Most of all, I hated getting home in the dark during the winter when the sun set at four-thirty. I couldn't go in the woods when it was dark.

We all adjusted fairly quickly to our new school. The only incident was a little boy who, not being familiar with the porcelain flush toilets, had a messy accident in his pants because he was afraid to use the bathroom.

Fortunately, Grandma and Grandpa Burns had indoor plumbing, so I was experienced with such things.

Chapter Twenty-Five

None of the communities served by Warba Elementary were what could be called ethnically diverse. Diversity in Blackberry meant having brown hair instead of blond. We were not all of the same nationality. I remember names like Gist, Erholtz, Larson, Erickson, Bently, Muechler, Bengston, Scott, Harju, and Brown. These represented Swedes, Norwegians, Finns, English, and Germans.

When I was transferred to Warba Elementary, I was not aware of the other students at first. We transplants from Blackberry School retained our autonomy for the remainder of first grade. We played together, ate together, and studied together.

The next school year, in the fall of 1950, I was in the mix with all second graders. Miss Warner hung back with the first graders.

Mrs. Sarja, my second grade teacher, called the roll. "Ahola, Aijala, Bently, Butts, Conely, Gould, Herschbach, Hietala, Huhtala, Korpi, Maki, Miatunen, Mostoller, Paralla, Williams." My new classmates were from communities named Swan River, Jacobson, Wawina, and of course, Warba. They were almost all of Finnish descent, many coming from homes in which Finnish was still the primary language spoken. Even my teacher spoke with a Finnish accent.

The differences between us were more subtle. I was from a family of miners and loggers, and many of my Finnish friends lived on farms. I came to school smelling like sawdust, they, like a barn.

Most of us arrived at school in work boots of some sort; I wore leather boots, laced up well above my ankles over a pair of wool socks. Many of my Finnish friends came wearing boots that were the precursor to today's fashionable Canadian felt packs. These boots had green rubber lower units to which were stitched leather uppers, and they too laced up well above the ankles. Into these boots were inserted heavy felt insoles. Add to that two pairs of wool socks, and a kid's feet were kept toasty warm.

I begged my parents for a pair of boots like those my Finnish friends wore. Mom and Dad insisted that wearing rubber boots indoors all day long would ruin my eyesight. What connection there could have been between my eyes and my feet, I'll never know. Anything my parents didn't want me to do carried with it the danger of having my eyesight ruined, even if it was having a second helping of pudding and eating it with a spoon.

"Mom, can I have a BB gun?"

"Dad, can I have a jack knife?"

"Mom, can I make a marshmallow toasting stick?"

The answer to all of these questions was always the same. "No, you'll just poke your eye out." I suspect that is why rubber-bottomed boots were bad for my eyes.

There were both pros and cons to wearing leather boots instead of rubber-bottomed packs. When I wore leather boots outside in winter, my feet froze, and I was sometimes in agony when I came in from recess and my numbed toes began to thaw. But after the pain subsided, the leather allowed my feet to "breathe," and they remained relatively dry. Then they were comfortable.

On the other hand, those who wore the green rubber packs on their feet were quite comfortable outside, even on the coldest days. But their feet would sweat, and when they came in from recess, the moisture was trapped by the rubber. Then they were the uncomfortable ones, forced to endure hot and sticky feet until they could go out and wade in the snow to cool down.

We didn't bring our shoes to school to exchange them for boots when we were outside because many of us didn't have other shoes. We were lucky to have a pair of canvas sneakers for summertime. Otherwise, we went barefoot.

I never did get rubber boots like those my Finnish classmates wore, and I still ended up wearing glasses.

Chapter Twenty-Six

Warba Elementary was large enough to offer a more diversified curriculum than Blackberry, yet small enough that I didn't get lost in the shuffle. By March of my second grade year, I was beginning to settle into my new surroundings. School started to become fun: especially recess. The playground was one large field bordered on the east by a road, on the west by a barbed-wire fence, and the south by a dense pine forest. There was a set of swings, a hand-pushed merry-go-round, and a slide.

In the spring when the snow began to melt in earnest, water ran in rivulets across the playground.

"Hey Jimmy, here's a good one," I yelled as I found a new rill running from a big puddle to another smaller one.

"Quick, dump more snow there," Jimmy said excitedly as we built the dam wider and higher.

"There's enough mud here to build it up. Look out! It's running around that side!" I sounded the alarm.

My classmates and I rushed around the playground, building miniature Aswan Dams wherever one puddle was emptying into another. We watched a head of water build up behind our barriers.

"Okay, I'm going to break it open now," John warned us.

He took the heel of his boot and gouged an opening in the slush-mud dam. The water rushed through the channel in a wave that "roared" down to the next puddle.

The Playground Regatta was born when we began to float small pieces of wood on our channeled rivers. We discovered that if we put our boats in at the impoundment created by our slush dams, they would be carried along with the flood. Since some boats went faster than others, that meant competition.

"Did you see how fast my boat went? Richard's is hung up on that clump of grass. Hey Dick, how's it feel to not make it to the next lake? Ha, ha!"

"Shut your mouth or I'll shut it for you. You just wait until tomorrow. Then we'll see who's laughing."

The next day Dick came with a crudely carved boat. Crude or not, it was a step up from what the rest of us had. Pointed at the ends and somewhat streamlined, it really didn't do any better than our pieces of sticks, but the challenge had been made.

Every day brought new and improved models to the waterways. We didn't pay much attention to what was being taught in the classroom for a couple of weeks each spring. All that mattered was recess when the yacht races began. They'd last until the bell ran, and then we would trudge reluctantly back into school, soaking wet. I hated having to sit in class with damp pant legs and wet wool socks.

Our activities were not so benign at other times during the school year. The playground equipment was rather meager. We had a swing set, but some of the swings were broken. The merry-go-round had to be pushed to make it move. Everything was made of steel, and the only padding was the bare ground. We invented ways to place ourselves in peril.

John got himself really dusted in snow one afternoon, making sure the seat of his pants was covered. He gingerly climbed the stairs of the slide so as not to lose any of his snow, sat down, and let go of the railing. With his snow-slick pants, he flew, hit the ground, and rolled over three times. Excited, the rest of us raced for the nearest snow drift to dust ourselves.

"Hey guys! You lift the snow crust real carefully, it comes up in a slab," I yelled, and I broke loose a chunk of crusty snow.

"Holy cow! Look at him go. I bet he flew five feet off the end!"

Another competition—who can generate enough speed coming down the slide to sail the farthest through at the end of the ride?

Soon the event was stepped up another notch. The snow banks by the parking lot faced south, and even in winter, the sun's rays could do some melting. But the wet snow froze as soon the direct rays moved. Chunks of ice formed.

Now the daredevils really came out to play. Peter broke off a chunk of ice large enough to sit on. He carried it up the slide and rocketed down on his icy seat.

"Hey Billy, I'll bet you don't dare do that standing up."

Billy made it about halfway down, fell over the side, and broke his collar bone. Someone ran into the school to find a teacher. I think the principal took Billy to a doctor.

Billy came to school the next day with his arm in sling, a hero. Unfortunately, the principal issued an edict that day. There would be no ice-riding on the slide. Another game had to be invented.

Depending on the season, we constructed baseball fields to start pick-up games. We played tag, wrestled, and fought. I didn't think twice about bringing my pocket knife to school.

"Wow, that's some jackknife you got there. Is it new?" John asked me.

"Yeah, Dad got it for me the other day. He said he was tired of me losing his all the time."

"Let me show you a game I play with my brother. It's called stretch." John made me stand facing him. "Now hold out your arm, and I'll do the same," he said. "Start with your feet together like this." John demonstrated what he wanted me to do. "Okay, open the biggest blade. When you throw it, if it sticks in the ground, I have to put my foot next to it. If you hit my foot, I win. When one of us is stretched out so far that we topple over, the other wins."

I threw the knife and stuck the blade six inches from his foot. He pulled it out of the ground and stuck it about the same distance from mine, and so the game went until I was stretched about as far as I could go. I began to lose my balance.

"Karen, you saw this. His hand touched the ground," John said.

"I couldn't tell. Do it again and I'll watch better this time."

And so the game went on. I won when my opponent left an indentation in my leather boot, just above my big toe.

I look at today's playgrounds with their paved surfaces, fancy slides, and swing sets over ground covered with a six inches of wood shavings, and I know that the playground supervisor would have a nervous breakdown if she observed what we used to do for fun.

Chapter Twenty-Seven

My education was important to my parents, and they encouraged me as best they knew how.

One season, I was to be the trunk of the Christmas tree in my Christmas program at Warba. I had one line of dialogue.

"We're sure glad you like school, Dennis," Dad said as we made the trip to the school for the event. "You know, when you finish high school, you can keep going to school. It's called college. If you go there, you'll never have to work in the mines like I do."

When we arrived at the school, I went right to my locker to hang up my coat. Carol Jean's locker was next to mine. "Guess what, Carol Jean?" I blurted out. "My Dad just told me that I get to go to college."

From that night on, there was no question about what I was going to do. Any conversation with my parents about the subject left little doubt. I was going to college. It didn't matter what I studied: I was going to college.

When I was older, many of my friends earned their way through college working in the mines. Dad never let me even apply. Ironically, he said the money was too good and the work too easy. Too many kids went into the pit and never left. Years later when I'd come home from college in the spring, he'd have some crappy job lined up for me. Between graduating from high school and my first year of college, he landed me a job with the county thinning stands of young pine in the woods. It was all axe work which wasn't bad. But he'd also purchased timber cutting rights from the county that summer. After my eight hours of chopping weed trees, Dad picked me up, and we went to the stumpage to cut pine logs until dark.

The second summer when I returned home, Dad had a job with a local contractor waiting for me. I wheeled concrete ten hours a day for a dollar and a quarter an hour. The third summer was the worst. A company called Nelson Roofing was hiring, and I went to work the day after school ended. I spent ten hours a day, six days a week, carrying boiling tar in five gallon pails, wrestling rolls of tarpaper, and sweltering in the heat on top of office buildings. By the end of summer, I could hardly wait to quit and go back to school. Dad made it clear there was no way I'd end up spending my life in a job like that.

Dad graduated from Greenway of Coleraine High School in 1936. He was a strong country boy who, amazingly, was one of the best javelin throwers in the nation. The spring of his senior year, he placed second in the state track meet. His technique improved so much that his distances increased by several feet each week. His high school coach entered him in several AAU meets where he competed against the best.

Dad saved his many ribbons and medals. I remember one memento in particular. It was the program for an AAU meet that had attracted the Big Ten champion and the winner of the Drake Relays. Dad had the gold medal for the javelin throw at that one.

He was invited to the Olympic tryouts that June, and his coach thoroughly expected him to move on. Unfortunately, not many days before the meet, Dad pitched a baseball game and injured his throwing arm. He took fourth the day of the Olympic trials.

"My coach wrapped his arms around me, wept, and said, 'We just lost a trip to Germany,'" Dad once told me. That was the same year Jessie Owens put in his remarkable performance in the sprints and the long jump.

I know Mom was proud of him. One June, for Dad's birthday, she bought a black picture frame and covered the cardboard behind the glass with deep-purple velvet. To this she glued his medals so they could be hung on the wall for everyone to see.

When he opened his gift, Dad gave his customary, "What the hell did you do that for?" Yet, when he died, he still had his framed medals tucked away in his bedside drawer.

Dad lost a lot the day he hurt his arm. His grades weren't great, and without his ability to throw the javelin, college was out of the question. That summer his father was killed in the mine, and Dad was the only son left at home. The responsibility of helping his mother and younger sisters fell to him. He was rooted in Blackberry.

Mom and Dad were overjoyed when I finished college. During a time when students were beginning to assert their rights, many refused to attend college graduation ceremonies as a protest against the establishment. But I would never have deprived my parents of the opportunity to see me walk across the stage and accept my diploma.

Chapter Twenty-Eight

"The principal has decided that since we have only a few days of school left, we are going to have a track meet tomorrow," my teacher announced. "Come prepared to run and throw and jump. There will be ribbons for prizes."

I couldn't wait to tell Dad. "Dad, they're having a track meet at school tomorrow," I said as soon as he came in the door.

"Really? Do you know what events they'll have?"

"First we'll do a sprint. Then we can broad jump and high jump, and then we're having a softball throw."

"Great. Let's go out in the driveway, and I'll show you how to start a sprint."

We went out and Dad demonstrated how to get down into the four point starting position and how to mark the spots where my feet were. Then he showed me how to dig small holes in the dirt so I could have toe-holds to push off. I was primed and pumped for the next day.

The call came for all fifth graders to report for the first event.

"Line up against the school wall," the principal instructed. "Your hand must be touching the wall."

I was not prepared for this, and all of Dad's coaching had to be ignored. As I was trying to assess the situation, I heard, "To your mark, get set, GO!" and everyone took off for the finish line. I was one of the last to make the break, but I ran as fast as I could to catch up. Everything became a blur as I strained to reach the finish.

"I've got number one!" the man hollered as he grabbed my arm. I had just won the sprint race. "Go over and tell the lady at that table you were first in the fifth grade sprint. She'll give you your ribbon."

I went up to the girl. "Hi, that man said to come over here, and that you'd give me my ribbon."

"What place did he say you took?"

"First."

"You get the blue one." I shoved it in my pocket because the broad jump was starting.

It was my turn, and I ran down the marked off runway and jumped.

"144 inches."

I watched the others jump. 120 inches. 132 inches. 110 inches.

"Where's the kid who jumped 144?" I stepped forward. "Go pick up your ribbon."

I went back to the lady at the table. "I won the fifth grade broad jump."

"No you didn't, I did," chimed in another voice. It was Daryl, the next closest competitor to my leap.

The lady looked at me. "How far did you jump?"

"144 feet."

"Yeah, right." She started to give my blue ribbon to Daryl.

"Wait! I mean 144 inches," I quickly added.

Luckily, the man who had been running the broad jump competition happened to walk by.

"Bill, which one of these kids won?"

"He did, the one who jumped 144 inches." I stuffed my second blue ribbon in my pocket.

I was off to the high jump. This was a cane pole suspended between two posts. The landing pit was a pile of sawdust.

"You again?" the woman asked as I approached for the third time. "What color ribbon are you picking up this time?"

"Blue."

I returned one more time after the softball throw.

"What place did you take," the woman asked, grinning. "First, I suppose?"

"No, I just got second this time, but that's okay. I didn't lose by much."

That night Dad came home from work, and I had my three blue and one red ribbon displayed on the table. He looked at them.

"What are these for?"

"I won the sprint, the broad jump, the high jump, and took second in the softball throw."

"How high did you jump?"

"I don't know, they didn't measure. It was just who went the highest."

"Well, how far did you jump?"

"144 inches."

"That's twelve feet you know. That's a good jump."

Then we sat down and ate supper. Later, after the dishes were done and Mom and I were alone, she gave me a long look. "You know, your father is very proud of you."

"Really?" I asked. It hadn't seemed much like it.

"Yes, he is." Mom patted my back.

It was nice what Mom said, but I wished I could have heard those words from Dad.

Chapter Twenty-Nine

Once or twice a week during the summer, after an early supper, Dad had baseball practice for the Blackberry county league team. He always took me with. We had two baseball gloves, both adult size, but I would put one on my hand and retrieve balls thrown back by the outfielders as they practiced catching fly balls.

Blackberry's baseball field left much to be desired. The outfield had a few boulders whose heads had been pushed to the surface by frost, and there were plenty of chuckholes a fielder could step in as he sprinted for a ball. The infield, although it was grass covered, was rough, and the base paths were only worn trails from base to base. Infielders always had to be alert for "bad hops."

Dad anticipated Sundays when the league games were played. In those days, almost every community in Itasca County had a baseball team. There were teams from Jacobson, Warba, Windego, Bena, Ball Club, Balsam, and Trout Lake, and the league was administered by Art Frick, a man devoted to the game. He drew up the schedules, made sure there were enough umpires, and maintained whatever semblance of order he could muster.

One Sunday, Blackberry was playing Jacobson. Uncle Wilfred was in centerfield for our team. The cleanup hitter for Jacobson stepped up to the plate and deposited the first pitch into the red pines behind my uncle in centerfield. There was no fence, so he rushed into the woods, looking for the ball. The runner madly ran the bases, and by the time Wilfred found the ball, dashed out of the woods, and threw it back into the play, the batter had crossed home plate—a home run. The second time Jacobson's cleanup hitter came to bat, he hit a resounding drive even deeper into the centerfield woods. Another home run.

Later in the game, between innings and before the cleanup hitter was to come to bat, Wilfred secretly slipped a baseball into his shirt and found his place in centerfield. The batter took a mighty swing and sent the ball soaring into the pines. This time, Wilfred sprinted into the woods and quickly removed the extra ball from his shirt. He stepped out of the woods, threw the ball to the cutoff man at second who wheeled and threw to home in time for the runner to be tagged out. Blackberry won the game by one run. Afterward, Uncle Wilfred confessed to Dad what he had done.

The last couple of summers we lived in Blackberry, Dad claimed he was too old to play anymore. He said he liked to go to the games just to watch.

"Come on, Gen. We're going to be late for the start of the game if we don't get going."

"Eddie, you're not going dressed like that, are you?" Mom asked rather disgustedly. "Those are the best clothes you own, and you know you're going to end up playing."

"No. Not this time. I'm too old to run the bases anymore. Let the kids play," Dad answered resolutely.

When we got to the field, the players were finishing their warm ups, and they came off the diamond to line a wooden bench near where we were sitting on the grass. One of them turned to Dad. "Ed, why aren't you suited up? If we win today, we win the county championship. We could sure use you."

"You know better than that," Dad answered. "You young guys are doing fine without an old man like me out there."

It was a tight game. In the bottom of the eighth inning, the score was tied, and Blackberry had two men on base.

"Ed, we need a pinch hitter. Come on and put on a jersey."

"See, I told you this would happen," Mom complained, but Dad went to bat anyway.

The first pitch was a ball, but the second was right down the middle of the plate, and Dad hit a screaming line drive over the shortstop's outstretched glove. Two runs scored, and Dad tried to stretch a double into a triple.

He saw that the play at third was going to be close, so he slid. "Safe!" the umpire called, and Dad was a hero. Blackberry won the game even though he was left stranded on base.

The ride home after the game was silent. Dad had some trouble working the clutch pedal because the sole of his left shoe was partially torn off. His skinned knee showed a hint of red through the hole he had ripped in his only pair of dress pants.

Mom didn't say, "I told you so," but she didn't congratulate him on a good game, either.

Chapter Thirty

Dad began coaching me as soon as he thought I was old enough to catch a ball. He gave me my first baseball lesson when I was five.

"I bought you a baseball and a glove," he told me one day when he came home from work. "No, the glove goes on your other hand. It fits pretty good. A little big, but not bad.

"Don't blink when the ball gets to you. Keep your eyes open. Now throw it back to me. No, don't throw it like a girl! Lead with your left foot and follow through—like this."

The ball sailed at me, and I jumped back.

"Don't step out of the way. It won't hurt you if it hits you. Hey, that was a good throw. Catch it now."

I winced. "Dad, that hurts my hand. Don't throw so hard."

"What do you mean it hurts? Catch it in your glove."

He threw it again, and I started to cry. This frustrated Dad. He came over and roughly stuffed his handkerchief in my glove. "Here, you baby, there's more padding. Catch this now." The glove bulged in the center, and that made it nearly impossible to catch anything. This ended my first lesson. I learned well—to not like baseball.

When I was a year or two older, we played a lot of catch. Dad was bound and determined I was going to be a pitcher, and he taught me how to throw a curve ball that would move away from a right handed batter or into a lefty. He showed me how to hold the ball so when it was thrown it would drop suddenly when it reached home plate, and he tried to teach me to throw a knuckle ball.

Most of the balls I had to play with were from the County League games, ones that had been hit so hard and so often the covers had been torn off. I picked up these discards after the games or practices, and Dad taped them up with black friction tape. Sometimes, in the woods behind the backstop at the Blackberry diamond, I'd find a foul ball lost during a past game. It would be water logged and heavy. I felt like I was throwing a shot put when I heaved it but (unlike the slippery black-taped balls that were my alternative) it had a leather cover and seams to grip.

When I grew older, I wasted too many years trying to be an athlete when I didn't have a chance. I was small for my age, one of the smallest in my class, and I wasn't terribly strong. That, coupled with my poor eyesight, meant I never developed into much of a player. I still blinked when a line drive was hit my way. My fastball was slow. I knew this disappointed Dad.

As a football player, I was pretty much a disaster. I froze when an opportunity came for me to make a big play. I missed crucial tackles, hesitated when I broke into the open on a run, or forgot plays. One time, though, I did make a spectacular catch at the close of a game. I leapt for the pass, gathered it in, and hung on as a linebacker bounced me out of bounds. In the same game I missed a tackle that allowed the runner to gain big yardage.

"Why did you miss that tackle?" was the first thing Dad said when I walked in the door.

When I was in my first year at Itasca Junior College, I went out for track for something to do. Genetics had worked wonders, and by this time I was six feet tall and weighed about 175. That spring I won the Northern Junior College Conference long jump.

I was still living at home, so when he came from work I said, "Dad, I won the long jump today."

He looked at me incredulously. "What happened?" he asked.

He seemed to think it must have been an accident that I'd won.

Chapter Thirty-One

Except for my one day of glory in fifth grade, I struggled to meet Dad's athletic expectations. Of course, I had other activities: reading and the woods. We had a few books at home, mostly Zane Grey and Jack London novels, and I started reading those after first grade.

When we were introduced to the library at Warba School, I was delighted to find it brimming with books and *National Geographic* magazines. I browsed through them during library period, pretending to not look at the pictures of naked native women. I took the books home and read at night. Reading was my passion, and I could hardly put a book down once I opened it.

"Dennis, it's your turn to help me in the copy room," Mrs. Gould caught me on the way out to the playground. "I know it's recess, but everyone takes a turn."

I'd been caught reading when I should have been working math problems, and I knew this was my penance. Reluctantly, I followed my teacher to the work room. Hardly big enough for two people, it had a short counter along one wall and shelves of blank paper ab-oe. The shelves on the other side of the room were stocked with miscellaneous supplies: pencils, a couple of extra blackboard erasers, and chalk. "Take this spatula and scrape out the old gel in this tray," Mrs. Gould instructed. "Put it in the waste basket. It's only gelatin and water."

"Okay, they're clean now. What's next?" I asked.

"We have to pour new trays for tomorrow. Here, I've mixed up this batch. You clean up if I spill."

Mrs. Gould poured the thick mixture into two trays and set them aside. "These are two trays I poured yesterday. See how they've set up? Just wait now, I have to put the master copies on them."

She had written on what looked like light green paper. There were two pages, and the second was coated with some kind of heavy dye or ink. Whatever she wrote on top of the green side transferred a mirror image on the backside of that page. "There, see how the ink dissolved into the gel?" I saw what looked like backwards writing on the surface. "Now take a clean piece of this white copy paper and carefully press it onto the gel. Then peel it back slowly. See how the printing comes off onto the paper?" Mrs. Gould stepped back. "Now you finish. We need twenty-four more copies," she told me.

I got to work. The first copy had vivid, purple printing on it. By the twentieth page, most of the ink in the gel had been used up, and the copies were getting faint. By my twenty-fourth copy, I could barely make out the faint bluish letters.

I finished just in time for class to begin and took my seat, listening enviously as my classmates discussed their recess adventures.

There were times during the school day, though, when I could let my imagination run wild. Some educational theorist had the idea that we would learn better if we were entertained, and movies made good entertainment. Most schools hadn't accepted this theory, and I don't think the idea ever caught on. In the next three years, after we moved from Blackberry, I attended several schools, and none of them showed as many films as I saw at Warba.

When it was time for geography class, we were ushered to the theater. There were a few rows of chairs on the stage behind the drawn curtain.

"Today, students, we are going to see a movie about Greece as a part of our geography lesson," Mrs. Gould instructed. "Greece is a country on the Mediterranean Sea, and it is a very interesting place."

The lights went out, and we were treated to underwater scenes of octopi and sponges. We saw narrow streets and rocky shorelines with boats moored to wharfs.

The movie ended and it was back to the classroom to read or answer questions about what we had seen. Later in the day we might see a movie about constellations for science class. Back in the classroom, we'd draw patterns of stars in the winter sky.

It seems that we spent more time watching movies than anything else. Sometimes we saw three or four movies in one day. I could sit in the dark and allow my mind to wander wherever it wanted to travel, never having to worry about being interrupted with a question or having Mrs. Gould notice that my eyes were closed and that I was daydreaming about some invention I planned to build.

Chapter Thirty-Two

The cafeteria ceiling of our school was low, and the floor was concrete. Long tables were arranged in rows. The menu lacked diversity and included ample servings of pasta, mashed potatoes, hamburger gravy, and plenty of rice. But what I remember most about elementary school lunchtime is my third grade teacher, Mrs. Gould, who escorted us to the lunchroom each day and sat with our class. She was tall with pitch black hair and a stern expression.

"John, take your elbows off the table, and Jim, sit up straight," she commanded. "Mary, use your fork. Rodney! Stop shoveling your food in as if your spoon is a scoop." Mrs. Gould turned her glare on me. "And Dennis, you will not be allowed to leave until you finish your milk."

I still had a dislike for milk, but that was because none of it was homogenized. Our lunchroom dose of cow-juice came in glass bottles, miniature versions of what creameries used to deliver milk to their customers. Each half-pint serving was capped with a cardboard top that had a pull tab protruding upward.

I looked through the glass bottle of lukewarm milk and saw the thick, yellow cream floating on the top of the skim.

"Hurry up now, Dennis. I'm not going to tell you again."

I shook the miserable stuff, mixing the cream as thoroughly as I could. Then in one motion, I pulled the tab on the cardboard cap, tossed it aside and, while holding my nose, I chugged the vile liquid as fast as I could, being sure to not breathe. But, no matter how long I held my breath and swallowed, when it was over, my mouth and throat would be coated with fat molecules. The taste would hang in my nostrils.

Not long ago, I visited Mrs. Gould. I heard she was living in the same assisted living facility as Dad, and I wanted to know if she had maintained contact with any of my classmates. An attendant pointed me to a table near the window. There sat one of the tiniest ladies I had ever seen. Her pure white hair was neatly trimmed, and her face was gentle.

I went over to her table and introduced myself, and when she looked up at me, I had the same feeling of apprehension I did when I was eight years old. She didn't seem particularly happy to see me, and when I tried to make conversation with her, her answers to my questions were short and to the point. She was not rude, just very businesslike.

After a few minutes she excused herself. She said she had an appointment she had to keep.

I could nearly taste the warm milk cream in my mouth.

Chapter Thirty-Three

At certain times of the year, the condition of our gravel country road made travel so difficult that school had to be canceled.

"Mom, when's mud vacation this year?" I asked every few days.

She answered the same way every time: "Probably not when we need it."

"How many days will we be out of school?"

"Same as last year, I suppose," she answered.

"Come on, Mom! Look it up for me. Will the snow be gone by then?"

"Why don't you go out and play in your snow fort? Spring will be here soon enough, and when it does come, mud vacation will be at the wrong time, like always. Now scoot!"

This conversation was prompted by an occurrence of which today's students can only dream, two weeks off from school for what was officially called mud vacation. Because of the way our country roads were built, the spring runoff pooled on the road surface, overflowed the ditches, and then soaked into the road itself when the frost left the ground. The receding frost also created frost boils, soft spots in the road that became bottomless pits of mud. A car would bog down to its running boards and come to a goopy, muddy stop. During those times of the year, the farmers and miners would park their cars at the Blackberry Store and walk home.

Almost all of us were bused to school, and I rode ten miles one way. Virtually the whole trip was on roads that were dusty in the summer and frozen solid in the winter. The only paved road in

Blackberry was Highway 2. Needless to say, school buses had no chance of completing their routes during spring breakup, and since our parents would never have allowed us to walk home from the highway, school was closed for a designated two week period every spring. It was named mud vacation, but it was a crap shoot if it would coincide with the actual muddy season.

What would happen was the school board, in planning the year's schedule, would set the date for mud vacation, and Mother Nature would set the date for spring breakup. We ended up with official mud vacation followed by a week or so of roads too muddy to travel, and our parents kept us home for that time as well. The extra days off were a complete bonus.

Not long ago, I took a drive around Blackberry, searching for the country road of my childhood, but I couldn't find one that even remotely resembled what I remembered as a child. Every surface was a two lane tarred road with white dotted lines delineating the center, and the ditches were dug deep. Wide mouthed culverts lay under driveways, more than ready to carry away the diluvial flow of spring. The sinkholes of spring have been rendered extinct, taking mud vacation along with them.

Chapter Thirty-Four

In Blackberry, there was little opportunity to attend Sunday school. In the 1940s and 1950s, the public schools provided time for religious education, but before we were old enough to attend school, Mom was the religion teacher for my sister and me. Each night she would tuck us in, and we prayed a simple bedtime prayer with her, "Now I lay me down to sleep." This, as well as saying Grace at every meal, became a ritual for us. I sat with Mom on the couch in front of the living room window while she made me memorize the Lord's Prayer. She also taught me Bible stories.

We had no church to attend in Blackberry. Because Mom didn't drive, we almost never went to church in Grand Rapids. I remember going once, on Easter Sunday, and Mom asked Dad a question on the way home. "Ed, don't you believe the Easter story is true?"

"No, I don't," he responded after a moment's hesitation. "How in the world could anything like that happen? I don't believe there is a God."

Dad never stood in the way of what Mom tried to teach us, and he always bowed his head for Grace and was respectful. He just didn't believe in religion.

Early in my second grade year, I came home from school with a permission slip. "Mom, the teacher wants us to bring this back with your signature if it's okay. All the other kids are going to do it because we get out of school for an hour. Can I?"

She read the letter asking permission for us to attend religious education sessions held at the Warba Town Hall once a week.

"What do you think, Eddie? Would it be okay if he went to these meetings? I don't know who this man is, but I'm sure he's all right if the school is letting him teach. It won't hurt Dennis to learn from someone else."

"It's okay with me. I guess it won't hurt him."

So, one Wednesday morning, everybody whose parents signed the permission slip walked the block to the town hall. Only a few in my class didn't attend.

The Reverend Herb Peters was a small wizened man with a voice like gravel, but he faced over a hundred rowdy students every week for the remainder of that school year. The town hall itself gave me the creeps. It had one large meeting room that was cold and drafty in the winter. However, the first impression was always the smell of mildew and aging varnished wood. Everything in the room was coated with dust. The Reverend would always start with a simple song, the kind sung at Bible camps, and we would have to try to follow along to unfamiliar words. Then he began the lesson.

"I knew a man named John Sorenberger, a truly evil man who was an outlaw of the worst kind. Even his father kicked him out of his house. He was a bad man. He drank alcohol, robbed banks, and fought.

"John was despised by everyone, and he was chased by the sheriffs of many counties in Minnesota until there were few places left where he could hide," Reverend Peters continued the story. "Finally John went into the deepest part of the forest."

This caught my attention. Surely anyone who wanted to escape to the woods couldn't be all bad.

"John worked in logging camps, staying to himself, and causing no trouble," Reverend Peters told us. "One day, a missionary from Duluth came to camp, and the loggers were ordered to listen up.

The missionary told the story of the prodigal son. John bolted from the room."

By this time I was enthralled. Certainly this logger, John Sorenberger, was indeed a prodigal son. I couldn't wait for the ending.

"When the missionary followed John outside and confronted him with his past sins, John fell to his knees and repented," Reverend Peters said, his voice becoming soft. "John Sorenberger became a missionary to the logging camps. He was such a good fighter that he would take unbelievers outside and beat them up until they accepted Christ."

A happy ending.

When he was finished, we sang a couple more songs before being dismissed to return to school.

Some forty years later I was reading a book about the missionaries to the logging camps and ran across an excerpt that went something like this:

By the nineteen forties the logging camps of northern Minnesota had all but vanished. The men who had toiled to bring the message of God to those wilderness camps moved into the communities of northern Minnesota. Men like Herb Peters continued their ministry in places without churches.

I may not have lived in a logging camp, but I realized that Herb Peters, the man who had come to teach a bunch of country children religion, was actually a missionary to us poor heathens of the hinterland.

Chapter Thirty-Five

The old pump organ in the corner wheezed when Dad's cousin, Amelia, began to pump the pedals with her feet; the tones emitted from its weathered pipes were more than a little off. Sometimes a key would stick, so the organ sounded like a bagpipe until the key was jarred loose. Often no noise came out at all. When that happened, it was up to us to fill in the the note that should have been there.

This was Vacation Bible school. Each summer, three or four young people in their late teens or early twenties would come to Blackberry to conduct two weeks of religious education. Some were seminary students who were fulfilling a requirement of their school, and others were lay people who were zealous in their beliefs. All were trying to save us. They were really quite nice and very enthusiastic about what they were doing. I suppose this was another missionary outreach program that I didn't know we needed.

"I want to bathe you kids tonight," Mom began. "Tomorrow you start Vacation Bible School."

"No way. I'm not going to school in the summer," I insisted.

"You are going, and I don't want any argument about it—period." Mom was firm. "It's held in the little chapel across from the baseball field. Give it a chance. You'll do fun things."

The next morning we were sent off to walk a mile up the road to the chapel, our bag lunches in our hands and a list of do's and don'ts in our heads.

"Hold your sister's hand all the way, and don't walk too fast. Remember, she's only five, so take care of her. Be careful crossing the highway."

Bible school was agony for me. To have to give up ten days of the summer: ten days of building lean-tos in the woods, ten days of shooting my bow and arrow at unsuspecting ground squirrels, ten days of freedom—it was akin to torture.

I had to trade that for ten days of being cooped up in a tar-paper covered building half the size of my classroom at Warba Elementary. And I had to sit quietly, looking wistfully out of the window at the fields and the red pine forests that surrounded the little chapel.

One day we were told to bring a bar of Ivory soap and a small knife. A knife! I thought things were finally going to get interesting. But when I arrived, thinking we'd be doing something outdoors with our knives, getting dirty and washing with our soap afterward, I learned we were going to carve a Bible out of the soap—indoors, of course.

I carved and pared, and then I examined my creation with a critical eye. It wasn't at all symmetrical. No problem. Just take a little off the other side to even things up.

Now it tilted the other way. My work continued: take a little here and a little there until eventually, I had the smallest and most lopsided Bible ever manufactured.

On the first day, the leaders had asked us to take a note home to our parents.

"Eddie, listen to this! We are expected to support the teachers as best we can." Mom's tone had a note of panic. "They need places to stay for the two weeks and places to eat. It says the first two nights they'll stay at Amelia's, but after that, they'd like to stay at other houses. We just don't have room for anyone here."

Dad spoke up. "Yeah, but they could eat a meal or two with us," he said surprisingly. "You could fix a pot roast with new potatoes and carrots from the garden or even one of your good hot-dishes. I know there will be some raspberries ready. We could have a raspberry pie for dessert."

"But look at this dump!" Mom lamented. "Do you actually want strangers to see how we live? I'm sure they are used to at least having running water and a toilet."

Dad was unmoved. "They use the outhouse at the chapel. And we've got an electric pump now. They won't mind. Anyway, if the kids are going to go to bible school, we should do our part."

"Look at this floor. What will they think when they see the holes in the linoleum?"

"Aw, please Mom, we'll help you clean," I offered trying to soothe the worry in her voice. "It'll be all right."

Eventually, Mom broke down and agreed to sign our family up to act as hosts for a couple of meals.

The first night the teachers came, tension knotted up my insides. Dad was uncomfortable because he didn't speak the language of religion, and he thought they would look down on him.

Mom was embarrassed because of the amenities she had to offer, especially when the teachers had to wash their hands in the basin by the kitchen sink.

But the meals were wonderful. Mom was an excellent cook.

During the days when our classes met, along with learning that I couldn't carve a soap Bible, I learned I couldn't sing songs and act out the words with hand and finger plays at the same time. I would turn red in the face, and beads of sweat would ooze out of my forehead. I stumbled through the motions, missing half of them and coming up three beats behind with all the rest.

One morning, when we were about halfway through our walk to the chapel, I saw a mother grouse with several chicks on our road. When she noticed us approaching, she spread her wings, and the whole covey of little ones crawled under. I walked slowly up to her and was amazed to see eight or ten little heads poking out from her breast feathers and under her wings. I watched them until we were getting late and had to move on. That is my favorite memory of Vacation Bible School.

Eventually, the two weeks were over. The missionaries packed up their accordions, their songs and hand gestures, their flannel boards, and the rest of their paraphernalia and moved on to another community where they could make life miserable for some other eight-year-old boy.

We got to keep our soap carvings of a Bible. What was left of mine after I whittled it away was good for one quick hand washing.

Chapter Thirty-Six

No matter how hard the missionaries and Bible School teachers tried, not everyone in Blackberry was a saint. The township had its share of "characters" who helped define our community.

Our neighbor, Pete, was basically a good man. He worked in the mines and farmed a few acres of land, though even to me it was obvious that his wife, Jane, did most of the heavy lifting. He worked on the haying and the plowing of the fields, mended fences and fixed broken machinery, but it was Jane who lugged heavy milk cans from the barn to the pump house for cooling, and it was she who fed the chickens and gathered eggs. It was Jane who milked the cows by hand and mucked out the gutters full of cow manure. Jane was a tough lady, and she could be tough on Pete as well.

One season, Pete set out to find a Christmas tree in the afternoon, hoping to get home before nightfall. Pete thought that stopping at the Blackberry Store with its attached tavern might be a good way to begin his hunt for the perfect tree. He'd just grab a quick shot of something to get him started. About midnight, Pete left the tavern without a tree, but he knew better than to show up without something for the family to decorate the next day. So, on the way home, he pulled over to the roadside ditch, cut a tree in the dark, and loaded it onto his car. Then he drove home and went inside to bed.

The next morning, Jane's voice came crashing down on his tender eardrums. With his head aching and reeling, Pete awoke to discover that he had cut down a scrawny jack pine—a weed tree.

The tree had about seven branches on it. One stuck out here, another there. The trunk was twisted and curled like an old man bent from toil. It was the sickest, most un-Christmas like Christmas tree that anyone in Blackberry had seen. Even Pete was mortified by the sight of the tree he had brought home, and he immediately began to pull on his boots to go to the forest to find a decent one.

Jane would have nothing of it. She made Pete put up the tree, and the family decorated it as though it were a majestic spruce, placing colored balls, bright lights, and tinsel on the few branches available. But no number of ornaments could change the fact that it was a miserable tree.

Pete's humiliation did not end there. Jane did an inordinate amount of entertaining that year, inviting neighbor after neighbor to their home, and everyone who looked at their tree gasped, "Why in the world do you have a jack pine for a Christmas tree?"

Jane's reply was always the same. "Tell them, Pete. Tell them why we have a jack pine for a tree this year."

Pete never cut jack pine for Christmas again.

Chapter Thirty-Seven

I only knew Mr. Hanson as a farmer, but even as a first grader, I understood that his religious beliefs came first. He belonged to a denomination that considered taking a life, even during war, to be morally wrong, and he was extremely devout in his belief. The night before Sabbath, Mr. Hanson would put out enough feed and water to carry his animals over the Holy Day, and during that twenty-four hour period, he did nothing but worship, meditate, and pray.

One day, I was telling Mom about the war heroes we were studying in school.

"Do you know who from Blackberry received the most decorations in the war?" Mom asked as she chopped vegetables for dinner.

"Is it Jerry? I bet it's Jerry, because he got shot. Is it him?"

"No, it's not him. It's Mr. Hanson."

"No way! All he does is farm and go to church. How can it be him?" I wondered.

"Mr. Hanson doesn't believe in killing, even in war. That's why he became a medic. They say he wouldn't even carry a pistol and that he saved many, many lives during the war."

"How did he do that?"

"When someone was shot, he would go out onto the battlefield and bandage them up. Sometimes he carried wounded men out to safety. He was quite a hero, but he doesn't take any credit."

I had a difficult time imagining this quiet man doing the things Mom said.

All the while Mr. Hanson peacefully worked his farm, another neighbor, Mr. Lehmann continued to fight his war, only this one was waged against an enemy he could never conquer—his memory. He had fought in WWII as well, but instead of saving lives, he had taken many. Mr. Lehmann landed at Normandy and fought his way up the bank to the breakout point and through the hedgerows of France.

Too often, Mr. Lehmann sat on a bar stool, drowning his memories in his beer. Finally, too inebriated to remember, he would stagger to his car and weave his way home—at speeds far exceeding those even a sober driver should have driven.

Mr. Lehmann and Mr. Hanson never met on the battlefields of WWII, but one evening they met on the highway. Mr. Lehmann, now totally numb to his feelings and his good judgment, was in his usual state of oblivion. He collided with Mr. Hanson at an intersection across the highway from the cemetery.

Mr. Lehmann killed five innocent people this time, including Mr. Hanson.

When I last saw Mr. Jimmy Lehmann, I was eighteen years old. Dad and I had cut saw timber that summer, and we needed someone to help us skid the logs out of the woods. Mr. Lehmann had a steel-wheeled tractor, so Dad hired him to help.

The first day he came to work, Mr. Lehmann's face was bloated and his eyes were red. He reeked of stale alcohol. The day was hot and the work demanding."Ed, I just can't go on today. I don't feel good," he said as he looked at Dad.

"Tell you what, Jimmy," Dad said as he looked Mr. Lehmann straight in the eye. "It's awfully hot today. We'll start early tomorrow when it is cooler."

"Thank you, Ed. Thank you." Mr. Lehmann was almost sobbing with gratitude.

"But," Dad continued, "you show up sober tomorrow, or you can take your tractor home."

Mr. Lehmann did come to work sober the next day, and he stayed sober for almost a week until the job was done.

Chapter Thirty-Eight

In the 1950s, the faraway Korean War affected even our small community. After I had just turned nine, I was home on a weekday during mud vacation when I heard an unexpected knock at our door. It was early in the morning, even before we had eaten breakfast, but Dad had already left for work. Because we were so isolated in the country, Mom was hesitant to open the door. "Who is it?" she called through the locked door.

"It's Mr. Parks," the man answered. "Can I speak to you for a moment?" Mr. Parks was an acquaintance of Dad's. Dad worked for him during harvest time when the oats needed shocking and threshing. The only contact I had with Mr. Parks was when I had trailed along with Dad on those work days, and even then, he was engrossed with getting his crop in and paid little attention to me. It was highly unusual for Mr. Parks to come to our house at any time, let alone before eight o'clock in the morning. Still, Mom felt safe enough to open the door: at least she knew who the caller was.

Mr. Parks stood in the entry. He was a small man, thin as a rail, and his shoulders sagged and added to the look of weariness created by the lines etched into his face. The tattered hat he held in his hands seemed to writhe in an effort to escape his grasp. "I was…I was wondering," he stammered. "That is, I was going to do some fox hunting down on the river bottoms today. I was thinking…could I take your boy with me? What, with the leaves not out yet, it's easy to spot the fox dens in the old river banks, and I, well, I thought maybe he'd like to come with. If it's okay with you."

I peeked around my mother at a man I had seldom seen and had never spoken to. Even so, I lived for hunting. I couldn't contain my excitement at the thought of going on a real fox hunt. "Please let me go, Mom," I blurted out. "It's just down on the river bottoms. Dad and I go there all the time."

"He'll be okay," Mr. Parks tried to reassure her. "We'll stay on my farm the whole time, and the missus has packed some food for us. I'll take good care of him."

Rather reluctantly, Mom gave her approval, and we drove off in Mr. Parks' beat up dark green 1930s Ford.

Mr. and Mrs. Parks lived about two miles down the road from us, and they farmed 160 acres of land bordering the Mississippi River. The river, as it meandered its way south, formed bends that were so sharp they seemed to fold over on themselves. We could stand on one bank, turn our backs to the river, and see the same river only a few yards across a narrow isthmus. But to follow the loop might be a hike of several miles. Eventually, the river would erode through this narrow strip of land and leave behind what was called an oxbow lake. Over time, the lake dried up, but the shape of the old river bed remained intact—this is what we called the river bottoms. Mr. Parks' land contained several of these features.

The Parks lived a simple life, one of the few families in our area that eked out a living by farming. They worked hard and seldom had time to visit neighbors, but they were always ready to lend a hand when it was needed. They had one child, a son, who joined the air force and who was a bomber pilot flying missions over the Thirty-Eighth Parallel in Korea.

All day long, Mr. Parks and I walked the river bottoms. It was April, and the place was really quite barren with only a few early ferns beginning to poke their fiddleheads above the soggy, brown leaves. Here and there, sweet colt's foot, one of the very earliest of wildflowers to bloom, was ready to open its honey scented flowers. With these conditions, we could see through the underbrush for some distance, and once in a while, we'd spot a red squirrel. A brilliantly colored male wood duck and his drab mate splashed in a pool. A weasel tried to slink away unnoticed, but he was still dressed in his white winter coat. He stood out strikingly against the brown.

We never really hunted that day. Instead we would walk a ways, then sit, and Mr. Parks would stare into the distance for a while. Then we'd get up and walk to another spot. That was not how I envisioned a fox hunt. At one stop, Mr. Parks spotted a rabbit about twenty yards away. "Do you want to shoot at it," he whispered.

I nodded, and he handed me the rifle.

"I think you were a little high with that one," he said after I missed my first shot. "Aim a little lower and you might get him."

I squeezed the trigger for a second time and waited for the rabbit to roll over dead. Instead, it hunched down a little closer to the ground. When the rifle was empty, Mr. Parks reloaded it for me. After I emptied the gun for the second time, the rabbit became tired of the game and hopped away, his white tail waving. "Well, you came close a couple of times," Mr. Parks said with little emotion in his voice. "Maybe it's best you didn't hit him. He's probably pretty skinny now that winter's over. Not very good eating." He looked down at me and smiled a sad sort of smile.

Eventually the sun began to set, and the purple hues of evening enveloped everything by the river. "We better be getting you home," Mr. Parks announced. "Your Dad will be back from work and wondering where we're at." We walked back to his house, climbed into the same rattling car, and drove home in the repeat silence from the morning.

When we arrived at my house, Dad was waiting nervously on the back step as he always did when I was late. I rushed into the house to tell Mom all that we had done, and Dad and Mr. Parks stood outside, talking quietly.

When Dad finally came into the kitchen, he scooped me up in his arms and hugged me far too long and far too hard, tears welled up in his eyes. Then, without a word, we sat down to supper.

Mr. Parks never came to take me hunting again. In fact, I don't remember seeing Mr. Parks until one evening several years later, when I was a teenager. My folks asked if I wanted to go visit the Parks'. They had moved into town, Grand Rapids, and I went along with my parents for something to do. Instead of acres of woodland, Mr. Parks "farm" was now a city lot. He had a wonderful garden, but instead of the Mississippi River running nearby, he had a garden hose. A cottontail rabbit lived under his step.

The adults had a good visit that night. I sat to the side and read a book. We were on the way home before I thought of my hunting trip with Mr. Parks. "Remember the day Mr. Parks came and took me fox hunting?" I asked Dad. "I wonder why he never came back to do it again."

Then Dad told me that only a few days before Mr. Parks took me to the river bottoms, a government vehicle had worked its way up the Parks' long driveway, avoiding the bumps and occasional rocks that had pushed their way to the surface that spring. An officer got out of the car and walked to the door, a telegram in his hand.

We regret to inform you that your son, Donald...

Mr. Parks had taken me to places he had shared with his son when his son was my age. He tried to relive his memories with me.

Chapter Thirty-Nine

"Say hello to Mrs. Johnson," Mom said once as we waited to buy groceries.

Before me stood a person with a gray crewcut, someone wearing a man's white tee-shirt and a pair of bib-coveralls with cuffs casually folded over a pair of work boots. I looked up in confusion, but I offered my hand obediently. "Hello, Mrs. Johnson," I said.

We left the store, and I was baffled. By all outward appearances I should have said, "Hello, Mr. Johnson," but then, of course, Mr. Johnson was standing right there next to the person I had addressed. To a seven-year-old, this was a significant dilemma. I wanted to be polite, but I also wanted to be correct.

As I grew a little older, I began to notice that, yes indeed, this person was a Mrs. After all, she had a husband named Pete, and they had children, although they were much older than I and were hardly ever around. The two, Mr. and Mrs. Johnson, seemed happy with each other, and they were very friendly to anyone who greeted them. I came to accept that Mrs. Johnson had a crewcut and wore men's clothing.

Mrs. Johnson and her husband owned the only other business establishment in Blackberry besides the Blackberry Store. The business area was small, smaller than many living rooms today, and the short walls were lined with shelves on which sat a few canned goods, a vinegar bottle or two, and a random collection of staples. There were a couple of five pound bags of flour, a few containers of salt and pepper, and three or four bags of sugar. If a person were stranded in a place like this, he would starve in a matter of days for lack of anything worth eating.

Behind the counter and to the right was the doorway to the couple's living quarters, blocked by a piece of heavy cardboard, much like the bottom of a double Dutch door. Curious, I once peeked over the top.

I gasped with shock.

In the kitchen, running as free as though they were on the open range, were about a hundred newly hatched chicks. They were hopping around pecking at pieces of chicken feed, drinking water, and dropping guano wherever they went. In the corner, a group of the yellow fuzz-balls sunned themselves under a heat lamp.

The stench streaming over the cardboard Dutch door made my eyes water. Mom and Dad had their differences about what clean meant, but in this case they were in total agreement. Raising chicks in your kitchen crossed the line.

In spite of their lack of business acumen, the Johnson's did no harm, and they were well liked in the community. The husband and wife duo lived for several years after my parents moved from Blackberry. I suppose Mrs. Johnson wore her coveralls to the end.

Not all of the residents of Blackberry were as interesting as the Johnson's. Most were just plain hardworking people.

I could look out our living room window and see for a quarter of a mile with nothing to obstruct my view. Across the plowed field, I could make out our nearest neighbors' home. Johan Schmidt, his wife, and their four boys worked the farm, although Johan held a regular daytime job as well. Johan and his family were good people and good neighbors by country standards. They mostly kept to themselves, but if we lacked a tool for a job and the Schmidts' had one, we knew we could ask to borrow it. If we needed help lifting a heavy object, they were there, willing to lend a hand.

Johan raised a few cows, maybe four or five, and a pig to be butchered in the fall. A few free-range chickens roamed the yard, and like everyone else in Blackberry, the family grew a huge garden to produce berries and vegetables that were canned each summer.

In the spring, Mr. Schmidt was in his fields until dark. He had to smooth the plow furrows, and with his tractor, he towed an implement called a disk harrow over the soil. Then he prepared the field for planting by pulling a drag with dozens of sharp spikes pointed downward across the ground. Most years he planted potatoes in that field, but some years he gave the soil a rest and planted either hay or oats. In the fall, he plowed under any weeds and plant refuse that lay on the ground, preparing the field for what had to be done after the snow melted. Year round, work occupied most of his waking hours.

For the adults, most activities revolved around work. There weren't too many opportunities to socialize in our rural community.

The exceptions were the dance halls. On Friday or Saturday nights, the halls were open, and beer was served to liven the place up. Many venues served mixed drinks as well, and it was customary for the revelers to have an open bottle of brandy stashed in the car. Sometimes dances were held in the haylofts of barns.

"Hey, Gen, there's a dance at Wints' place," Dad announced when he came home from work one Friday night. "What do you say we go? My sister will babysit the kids."

"You know I don't like those dances," Mom reminded him. "People get drunk and there's always a fight. I feel out of place."

Mom didn't drink alcohol, and she always said she couldn't dance. I don't think that was true. She was just too self-conscious to get out on the dance floor. Dad, on the other hand, loved to dance, and Mom said he was really good. He didn't mind having a drink or two, either, and because of his size, he wasn't easily intimidated by those who came to start a brawl.

"Come on Gen," Dad persuaded. "We don't have to stay late. We'll be out of there by the time things get rowdy."

"Promise me we'll leave early and I'll go."

"I promise." Dad smiled.

Adults talk—children listen. The trouble is adults sometimes talk at the wrong time, or children listen when they shouldn't be listening. At any rate, after a night at the dance hall, I was privy to the knowledge that after he had drunk a few too many beers, our neighbor Johan Schmidt was very adept at unhooking ladies' garters from their silk stockings when he was dancing with them. More often than not, he woke sporting a blue-black "shiner" after a night of dancing.

For 165 hours out of the 168 in a week he was a quiet, respectable man, but on the dance nights, Mr. Schmidt sometimes lost it.

Mr. Schmidt would let me watch with morbid fascination when the pig was killed in the fall, its meaty throat cut from ear to ear. Through witnessing this spectacle, I learned that death is final and sometimes messy, and that it was no small thing to kill an animal. I also learned that we have a responsibility to not take lightly the death of even an animal we used for food. I didn't want to see the pig suffer, and I wanted its death to be quick and clean.

I knew where our food came from. It was not a process sanitized by walking into a grocery store and buying a package of precut pork chops. The pig's blood, as it gushed from the gaping wound in the animal's throat, was collected in a large basin to be used for blood sausage, and when they eviscerated the animal, the liver, heart, and kidneys were saved for cooking. I watched as Mrs. Schmidt placed the intestines in a pail of water to be cleaned and saved for sausage casings, and I helped shave the bristles from its hide so the hams and bacon would have a rind on them after the meat had been cured in a smokehouse.

Mrs. Schmidt rendered the fat to make pure white lard that would find its way into pie crusts, and even the head of the pig was boiled in a large vat. Later, the skull was picked clean, and whatever had been gleaned from the last of the poor animal's remains was pressed into lunch meat called head cheese.

I learned a valuable lesson from the Schmidt family: if we are going to eat meat, something must give up its life. And if an animal is going to give up its life for our sustenance, we better not waste what it gives us.

People living in Blackberry were pragmatic about life. They did what they had to in order to survive.

Chapter Forty

Dad got along with most of the people in Blackberry, but not all of them. One day he stormed into the house after work. He was so agitated he could hardly sputter.

"That crooked bugger down the road!" Dad ranted. "That miserable excuse for a mechanic, do you know what he's been doing? That bugger's been putting a 500 watt light bulb under the hood of that damn Chevy every night. No wonder the damn thing has been starting every morning. And then he goes around telling half the state that his car starts better than mine. Well, no wonder it starts every morning; he's wasted enough electricity to light up half of Blackberry, and then he has guts enough to brag to everybody that his Chev is so damn good!"

According to Dad, there were only two makes of automobiles: Fords and the rest of the junk people drove. Vic, the neighbor who lived a mile or so down the road, held the same philosophy—reversed. His choice was Chevrolet. How two grown men could hold such carved in granite ideas about something as purely functional as an automobile, I'll never know, but this difference in preference led to a feud that lasted for years.

Both Dad and our Chevy-loving neighbor Vic worked in the Danube Mine, but there was no way they would carpool. Instead, every morning they'd go out to their individual cars and work at bringing them to life. Often during the winter the temperature would drop to below zero, sometimes as low as forty below.

If one or the other's automobile didn't start, the owner had to have a hearty breakfast of crow and then call the neighbor to ask for a ride to work. That was the humiliation of all humiliations, to have to admit to the other that his car wouldn't start.

Unlike Dad, Vic had a sort of garage, so it was indeed sweet those mornings when Dad would receive a call asking for his assistance. Then there was a streak of frigid weather when Vic's car started no matter the temperature outside. That's when Dad found out about the light bulb.

His rampage went on for a good ten minutes, but the animosity went on for years.

Chapter Forty-One

I spent most of my childhood riding in old rattletrap cars.

I vividly remember the smell of these old heaps of rusted metal and loose bolts. It was a cross between mildew, dust, and a third ingredient that I can't quite put a finger on, something like the odor of fabric that had sat in a closet for years. When the sun shone on the car and the temperature inside rose to near 100 degrees, the aroma lifted up like a specter buried deeply within the seat cushions. Perhaps the reason for the smell was that our cars were always about a decade behind the current date.

Because the Mississippi River bisected Blackberry Township, there had to be a bridge, and the Blackberry Bridge spanned the expanse of swiftly flowing water. We lived only a short distance from the river's headwaters of Lake Itasca, about sixty miles as a crow flies. Even that close to its beginning, the river was some thirty yards wide.

The bridge had been rebuilt in the 1920s. Originally, it was high enough to allow steamboats to pass under. Ironically, after the high-bridge had been built, only one steamboat made its way to Grand Rapids. After the riverboats quit running, the decision was made to lower the old high-arching bridge. When my father was a child, he lived only about a quarter mile from the bridge. He was there to watch construction workers lower it to its new level.

"See how high the arch is to this bridge?" Dad told me once while the two of us drove up to the approach of the remodeled bridge. "That's how high the roadbed was before they lowered it."

I wanted him to tell me about when they brought the old bridge down to this level.

"First, they raised it up and cut the abutments," Dad explained. "Then they lowered the whole thing down onto them, to where it is now. Before they finished it, me and the Bengston boys would crawl out on the bare beams. We'd sit in the middle of the span and chew tobacco and try to spit on stuff that was floating down the river."

I stared at him in disbelief. "Didn't Grandma and Grandpa get mad at you?"

"Naw, they were too busy to notice, but you'd better not try a stunt like that."

I wasn't allowed to sit by the river by myself, let alone walk steel girders suspended twenty feet above the water. At any rate, I probably wouldn't have done what he did. Whenever we crossed that bridge, I was scared like I was on a Ferris wheel stopped on the very top. When I was in the front seat, I had the urge to reach over and stomp on the gas pedal so we would get the agony of a slow death out of the way.

The remodeled bridge was a span only wide enough to allow a single automobile the size of a Model A Ford to cross. It was made of steel beams and girders that arched high overhead with crisscrossed steel I-beams that kept everything from swaying from side to side and up and down.

But the thing that made traversing this span so frightening was the wooden planking of the bridge. Three-inch thick slabs of wood made up the deck. Some of them had knotholes you could see through, and some were half rotted. They were not bolted down, so they were free to dance around as a car trundled its way across. The racket was almost deafening, like the din of a thousand trolls banging on metal garbage cans as we crossed. If I peeked out the side window and looked down, I could see through the cracks in the roadway to the river twenty feet below.

I had childhood nightmares of that bridge, and they always ended up with me falling.

Several years ago, the Blackberry Bridge was torn down and replaced with a new, modern concrete structure wide enough for two trucks to meet in the center and pass each other. It has no steel canopy over the top to amplify the sounds of clattering boards, even if there were any boards there to bounce up and down.

Besides the racket from the bridge, our cars were rattletraps themselves. They were often third or fourth hand, and the vehicles were subjected daily to a continual hammering and shaking from the condition of the roads. Like all country roads, ours developed washboard ripples. Dad insisted that the way to alleviate the discomfort of the bumpy roads was to drive fast.

My sister and I would sometimes pretend to be singing opera when we went over the washboard roads, singing the sounds of the scale by saying "AAAAH." The rough road took care of the rest and produced a most exaggerated vibrato that would have made any virtuoso jealous.

It was worst if I had forgotten to go to the bathroom and my bladder was full. My parents would say, "You can wait until we get home," and I'd cross my legs and sweat as the car convulsed up and down. I yearned to be able to stand behind one of the jack pine trees in the ditch and water it. Luckily, I always made it home.

Eventually, the road became so rough it had to be graded. This happened when the township had the funds, which wasn't often. The grader had four metal wheels, no engine, and a tongue attached to a farm tractor which pulled it on its task. The operation took two men: one to stand on a platform at the back of the contraption and to control the grader blade, and the other to drive the tractor.

It is the tractor driver I remember most vividly. Big and fat, he moved with the speed of a slug and even resembled one in shape. Most tractors have hand operated throttles that stay in position until moved either up or down to another notch, and this driver would set the throttle, lean back as far as he could in the seat, and tilt his cap over his face. Then he would put his feet in the spokes of the steering wheel and steer an erratic course with his clodhoppers. Perhaps this is why our road never had a proper crown in the center and why there were always ruts and ridges to catch the tires of cars.

Maybe this is why my aunt Bertha, who drove her 1940 Chevrolet much too fast and never with both hands on the wheel, ended up in the ditch so frequently. At least the road to her house passed through a muskeg swamp, so she had a soft landing when she went off the road. Aunt Bertha was German, heavy-bodied and muscular, and she wore her hair in long braids wound around her head. After she put her car in the ditch, she would have to walk to find someone to help her pull her vehicle back onto the roadway.

The neighbor's team of Belgian work horses came to know Aunt Bertha well.

Chapter Forty-Two

One day in 1950, Dad announced that he didn't think our old junker could be repaired anymore. He had his eye on a new car on the dealer's lot, robin's egg blue with a three speed manual shift on the column and a ninety horsepower engine.

"Do we really need a new car?" Mom asked. "I was hoping we could get linoleum for the floors."

"We do." Dad told her. "The one we have is about to give up the ghost. I've never had a new car before, and it sure would be nice not to have to be fixing it every day."

"It seems like a lot of money for us to put out right now."

"Well," Dad began, speaking slowly. "I figure things are pretty good right now. We've just signed a new contract at the mine."

Miners lived under the threat of a strike. Every few years, their contracts expired, and negotiations were held in Cleveland or some other eastern city. More often than not, the company and the union couldn't reach an agreement, and union officials elected to strike.

"The new contract runs for two years," Dad rationalized. "We don't have to worry about another strike until then."

Dad was about to break his own rule of never borrowing money. Instead of securing a bank loan in Grand Rapids, Dad decided to ask Thor and Torkle Ingstead if they would lend him the money. One Saturday morning, he went to their home. After a very brief conversation, Torkle went upstairs and returned a few moments later with a fist full of bills crisscrossed in his hand. There was little formality as far as paperwork and no need for a background check in our small community.

The Ingstead brothers were among the most well off people in Blackberry, and they were extremely generous. They had two teams of work horses which they used for farming, and Dad borrowed them, no questions asked. He used them to dig the basement for our house, to clear land, and to break the top soil for planting.

Torkle was in charge of the farm. He was the one who rose early and hitched up the team of horses to the plow, the seed drill, or the harrow. It was Torkle who walked behind his team, whistling to them or guiding them with the reins until it was breakfast time.

Thor didn't work the farm much. He was a railroader and was gone a good measure of the time. I never saw him dressed in anything but his bib coveralls and a blue work shirt, and he always wore leather work boots.

The two of them, Torkle and Thor, made quite a team. They were stalwart members of the community, they worked hard, and at harvest time, they provided jobs for many who needed them.

However, Thor did have at least one bad habit: he chewed tobacco, and he'd spit the juice wherever he was, whether indoors or on the street. Thor once walked into the Cadillac dealership in Grand Rapids, dressed as always in his work boots and bib coveralls. It took quite a while for the salesman to realize that Thor was not going to leave, so he walked over to that hillbilly of a man.

"Can I be of some assistance, sir?" the salesman asked.

Thor spit on the highly polished terrazzo floor.

"How much for dat car over dere?" he asked, and he pointed at a new Cadillac on the showroom floor. Then he spit again.

"That model sells for $3,500," he said, confident that Thor would leave after hearing the price.

Thor reached into his bib coveralls and pulled out a wad of bills. As he peeled off layer after layer, he said matter-of-factly, "Vell, I tink I'll take it den."

Then he spit on the floor.

Suddenly the salesman couldn't move quickly enough. Thor left with what remained of his money, his wad of tobacco, and his Cadillac.

It was an exciting day when Dad bought our new blue Ford with the money he borrowed from the Ingsteads. He drove it into the yard and lifted the hood so he could examine the shiny six cylinder motor. While he admired the engine, Janice and I climbed into the back seat and inhaled the new car smell, and Mom sat in the front seat to check if the swing-down visor would shield her eyes from the sun. As was the case with every car, she was too short, and the sun hit her in the face.

"Couldn't you find one with an adjustable visor?" she complained. "I'll never be comfortable this way."

Dad rolled his eyes at the sky.

Chapter Forty-Three

"Wow, look at the snow come down. Do you think we'll have school tomorrow?" I asked excitedly.

"I think you can stop dreaming," Mom said, dashing my hopes. "The snow isn't sticking to the road. See, the flakes are melting as soon as they hit the ground."

We were riding home from Grand Rapids, and the beams from our headlights pierced the darkness and illuminated the snowflakes so they looked like millions of white needles hurling at us. And Mom was right. When I woke the next morning, those few early flakes had all disappeared, and I had to get on the school bus.

When I was a boy and the first flakes of a snow came drifting down, the adults prayed it wouldn't be a real blizzard. If it did become a full fledged storm, then they hoped they had enough food in the cupboard to last a day or two, sometimes more. This was because once the snow started, there was no hurry to clear the roads. What sense did it make to rush out and begin plowing if the job would just have to be repeated when the storm ended? We waited, knowing that eventually the men who drove the snowplows would reach our road.

Those plows were dump trucks loaded down with a heap of sand in their boxes. They were equipped with plows shaped like a V. These V-plows were marvelously efficient at breaking through drifts, and they cleared the roadway slick and clean.

The drawback with a V-plow was that it left two snow banks, one on each side of the road. With each successive plowing, the banks grew higher. Each time it snowed, if there was only a slight wind, the road drifted level from bank to bank. Then the plow came by and piled the banks higher yet. It didn't take long for the banks to be several feet high in places, which meant that after a snowfall, the road could be blocked by many feet of drifting snow.

That is when the V-plow excelled. Their engines would be revved up, the transmission would be shifted into the "bean hole" (the lowest gear possible), and the mass of steel would be slammed like a battering ram into the drift. Often it took two, three, or several charges at the concrete-like white stuff for the plow to break through.

"Mom, when do you think the plow will be going through?"

"Well, it stopped snowing early this morning, so I guess it should be any time now." Mom was less excited about the plow than I was. "Keep watching for it, but I don't want you anywhere near when they're plowing. You know that one of the kids on the other side of the river was buried in snow last winter and almost died."

"Hey, there it is. Look at the banks he's piling up. He's by now. Can I go out?"

The first thing I'd do once Mom let me out was climb the mountain of snow that had been pushed aside by the plow. Then I'd get a shovel out of the garage. It was time to do some serious tunneling. I'd dig into the bank a few feet, and then I'd begin to enlarge the hole to make a room. Sometimes the cavern became large enough for me to comfortably sit upright. That was when I started to dream about being stranded in the wilderness.

After a trip to the house to gather a candle, some matches, and an old throw rug, I'd retire to my snow retreat and set up house-keeping. I'd light the candle, spread out the rug, and lie there—pretending I was warm.

At some point, a transportation engineer realized that if we were to eliminate the high snow banks piled up by the V-plow, the roads would not drift shut. The wing-blade was invented to solve this problem. V-plows mounted on the front of the truck were replaced with diagonal blades that rolled the snow in only one direction. Then it was picked up by the wing-blade and pushed entirely off the side of the road. So, no banks, no drifts.

I wonder now if we really had that much more snow when I was a child, or if it only seemed that way.

Chapter Forty-Four

KA-WHOOMP! That is the sound a shotgun makes when fired point blank into a lake. I know that because I sat next to Dad on the lake's bank when he shot fish.

I was only five when Dad took out his twelve gauge shotgun and asked me if I wanted to come for a walk. Never one to turn down an invitation to accompany Dad when he had his shotgun in hand, I eagerly skipped along beside him. I wondered what we were going to hunt. I knew that grouse and duck seasons were in the fall, and I couldn't think of anything else we'd be after.

It was a wonderful warm day in late April, and as we walked through the jack pine forest, I could smell spring in the air. Sedges that grew like grass in low areas were beginning to sprout. They gave off a minty smell when we stepped on and bruised them. This aroma mixed with the smell of damp soil and rotting leaves. We found a patch of pink flowering Arbutus, and Dad stopped to have me smell its delicate perfume that was sweet and almost fruity. Mixed in with them was wintergreen, and he told me to pick a leaf or two to chew on. There were even a few leftover waxy wintergreen berries to eat, and we savored the fresh minty taste.

Then we continued our walk, skirting around the swampy end of Arvid's Lake. When we reached the other side, Dad sat down on the grassy bank and stared into the water.

"What are we hunting, Dad?"

Dad shushed me. "Just sit very still. We don't have to talk all the time when we're out here, you know."

I sat like a statue.

As we rested there in the peace and quiet, a ripple broke the calm surface of the lake. Dad raised his shotgun to his shoulder and fired.

KA-WHOOMP! The water spouted up and something white floated up in front of us. I recognized it immediately—the white underside of a fish.

Dad waded out in the shallow water and retrieved a northern pike. Even as a child, I knew this was definitely illegal. Number one, fishing season was three weeks away, and number two, a twelve gauge shotgun could never be confused with a rod and reel. But we had fish that night for dinner.

Buffalo fish live in the Mississippi. Some weigh fifty pounds or more, and their scales can be as much as an inch in diameter. I always thought they resembled carp, but they are in a different fish family. Usually considered inedible, my Blackberry neighbors found that when they were salted and cooked in a smoke house, buffalo fish are quite good eating.

In the spring, when the river flooded its banks and filled the oxbow lakes, the buffalos gathered in the shallows to spawn. Mr. Parks owned land that contained one of these lakes. Every spring after the fish had come in to spawn, he'd stretch a length of chicken-wire fencing across it, cutting off any escape to the river. There would be hundreds of fish trapped behind that mesh. Then, all of the neighbors would get together—with their guns of course—and begin shooting fish.

At the end of the day, hundreds of pounds of fish would be ready for the smokehouse. In this case, it was perfectly legal because buffalo fish are considered "rough" fish with no closed season. I'm not too sure about the guns, however.

The buffalo fish were shot because their scales were so tough that spears had a difficult time penetrating. Northerns and walleyes were different. They were speared and taken home. We ate them that same night.

One spring, Dad and Uncle Hub went spearing suckers, another rough fish, which were gathering in a nearby stream to spawn. As usual, I'd tagged along with Dad. Uncle Hub and Dad were wading in the stream, looking for the shadowy figures of suckers as they darted out of the way. I became bored with watching them, and when a meadow vole went scurrying by, I gave chase. It disappeared in the tall grass next to a pond the size of a small swimming pool. I bent down to look into the water, and the surface erupted into a melee of splashing fish.

It seems the creek had been so high during spring runoff that it and the pond had been linked. During that time, the suckers had migrated to the site. Then the water level dropped, and the fish were trapped.

"Dad! Uncle Hub! This thing is filled with fish. I can see them swimming all over the place."

The two men came running with their spears, and they waded out into the thigh deep water.

"There goes one. Get it!" Dad hollered.

"Ah heck, they're so darn fast I throw behind them every time!"

Dad was standing in the middle of the pond. "Now the water's so muddied up I can't see a thing," he complained. "I can feel them hitting my legs, but I can't see them. Dang, I missed another one."

Luckily, Uncle Hub had brought a gill net along. He and Dad used it as a seine to dip the fish out of the pond, and soon suckers were flopping all over the bank.

"Hub, look at those fish. Not one of them has a spear mark in it. If Bolsdorf stops us, he'll know for sure we netted them. We better make it look good."

"Dennis, jab each one of them in the back with my spear. Make sure you don't stick them from the belly side. He'd spot it right away, and no fish swims upside down. Get going now."

John Bolsdorf was the game warden, and even I knew we didn't want to get caught netting fish illegally. That evening, I speared about fifty suckers, each right behind the gills. If we had been stopped by Bolsdorf that night, I wonder what he would have thought of the spearing skills of Uncle Hub and Dad?

Another fine spring evening when I was a year older, Dad asked if I wanted to take a walk to the other side of Arvid's Lake. I was happy to go, of course. When we arrived at the creek that connected Arvid's Lake to the river, we sat down for a while, which puzzled me because it was almost dark. Then I saw our neighbor, Vic, coming down the bank on the other side of the creek.

"Hi Ed. How's it going?"

"Pretty good. What do you think of this weather? It sure is warm for mid-April. I could sit all night and listen to the running water."

Vic stooped down and picked up a small rock from the dirt, and he tied something to it. Then he tossed it across the creek. "What shift do you work tomorrow? Afternoons?"

"Yeah. I suppose that means I can sleep in tomorrow, unless something comes up." As he spoke, Dad went over and picked up the rock Vic had tossed across to our side. Attached to it, I could see a piece of black-woven fishline. Dad began to pull the line, and after going hand over hand a couple of times, a stronger piece of cord came to us. Then I saw a square hook begin to stretch across the creek.

"Square hook" is a euphemism for gill net. This is a web made of gossamer thread woven so the mesh is large enough for a fish to stick its head through but too small for its body. When the fish tries to back out of the net, its gill covers get caught in the net, and it can't go forward or backward. It's trapped.

When the net was anchored, Dad said to Vic, "Gotta go. See you tomorrow," and we headed home in the dark.

When I woke up the next morning and came into the kitchen, Dad turned to me. "What did you think of that fish last night?" he asked.

I was confused. "What fish?"

"Don't you remember the fish I showed you?"

"What fish?" I asked again. I could remember setting the net but that was all.

Eventually, Dad realized I had never really been awake when he got me up after he checked the net. He had carried home a monstrous northern pike that I'd looked at and never seen. By morning, he had already cleaned it, and the pieces were stacked in our refrigerator.

Chapter Forty-Five

Dad once invited me to help him catch frogs.

"Sure," I agreed immediately. "But what are you doing catching frogs?"

"I thought we'd go fishing today. We'll use the frogs for bait," Dad told me.

"I thought the season didn't open for a few weeks," I said, puzzled.

"We'll just go lay on the river bank in the sunshine. No one will bother us down at the creek."

We caught a half dozen leopard frogs in the shallow water of the lake. Dad put them in a quart jar he had brought along. We walked around to the other side of the lake, crossed Al's pasture, and made our way down the river bank.

"Here's what we need," Dad said as he eyed a stand of willow saplings. He cut two sticks that were about seven feet tall. "Now we tie the line to the poles." He took a skein of heavy green fish line out of his pocket. The label said "50 lb. test." "Tie it tight around the butt end of the pole. That's right: now string the line about two feet toward the pole's tip and loop it around the willow. Then go up two more feet and do the same thing."

By this time I was beginning to catch on, and when I reached the tip of the willow, I had a pole rigged up that would evenly distribute any tug on the end of the line the full length of my makeshift rod.

"Let's tie a hook on the line. Then we'll be set to fish," Dad said. He added a lead sinker. I watched intently as he impaled one of our frogs on the hook, and it kicked to free itself. I didn't like this at all. The frog was much bigger than a minnow or worm, and it looked like it hurt when the hook punctured its lip. But then Dad lobbed it into the river current.

He took both of our willow poles and jammed them deep into the mud of the river bank. We lay back in the grass near the river, keeping one eye on the tips of our rods while we dozed in the warm spring sun. We talked some, but mostly we looked at the few clouds in the sky as they drifted by, and we listened to the birds as they challenged rivals for the best nesting spots. I watched the water move, saw eddy currents that formed like miniature tornados and then spiraled down into funnels, snatching unlucky insects from the surface.

The day was so calm, so peaceful, that I didn't even think about exploring or chasing animals. I don't even remember what we caught that day. I was just happy to be there with Dad, waiting for the fish to bite.

That spot where the creek joined the river was a favorite fishing spot for us during the legal times. Dad brought his ancient bait-casting reel that sounded like a miniature thrashing machine when he flung the bait into the river. I had my genuine cane pole bought at the Ace Hardware Store in Grand Rapids, threaded with the same heavy green line we used on the willow poles.

Because we weren't sneaking around this time, Dad had bought bait on his way home from work the night before, and he had a dozen minnows. With minnows, we usually caught enough fish for supper, either walleyes, northern pike, or both.

"You're not doing that right," Dad told me. "Hook the minnow through its tail. Here, give me that. You're never going to catch a fish that way." Dad took over. He jammed the cane pole into the bank. "Now watch your bobber. If it's pulled under, grab the pole and haul in the fish."

I sat next to the pole, waiting. Suddenly, the red and white bobber started sinking under the water, a sure sign that a walleye was taking the bait.

"Dennis, you've got a bite! I'll help you so you don't lose it."

Before I could pick up the pole, Dad jerked it out of the bank and set the hook. With one sweep of the rod, he flung a two pound walleye up on the bank. He unhooked the fish and threw it in the grass on the river bank. When we got home, he held up the fish for Mom to see. "Look what Dennis caught. We have fish for supper tonight." I didn't tell Mom I hadn't even touched the cane pole.

If the fish weren't biting, we could always engage in another favorite pastime by the river—clam throwing. When I got tired of fishing, which usually happened after a half hour or so, I waded in the river where a sandbar had formed, and with my bare feet, began to feel around for clams. Once I located them, it was only a matter of reaching into the mud and pulling them out. I'd dig a shallow holding pond in the sand near the river and store the clams there. When I collected a few, Dad and I began trying to throw them across the river. The clams Dad threw would reach the far bank, but mine always fell short. I never did tire of trying, though, and before we moved from Blackberry, when I was ten years old, I finally landed one on the other side of the Mississippi. It felt like a rite of passage.

As much as I liked fishing, I never enjoyed eating the fish we caught. That had to do with the preparation. Most people in those days didn't approve of filleting fish because they said it wasted too much meat, and the fish were cleaned in a way to preserve every morsel.

Mom would yell at Dad when he tried to clean the fish in the house. "Get those smelly things out of my kitchen! You're not going to scale them in here. The last time you did it took me two weeks to get rid of all the scales."

When we scaled fish, the scales flew everywhere. Mom would find scales stuck to the cabinets, the floor, even the ceiling. No matter where we cleaned the fish, we ended up with scales on our clothing and in our hair.

"Come on, Dennis," Dad said, giving in. "We'll have to clean them on a plank outside."

Kneeling before the plank, Dad showed me how to scrape the fish with a knife blade. "Now make sure you get all the scales from around the fins," he told me.

After the fish were scaled, we gutted them, cut their heads and fins off, and finally cut them into pieces. Dad made no attempt to rid the meat of bones. He simply cut the fish like pork chops off a loin.

"You kids be careful when you're eating this fish," Mom said. "I heard that John Jarvi almost choked to death last week when he got a bone stuck in his throat. Let me break it up for you."

The fish was minced, and we were forced to take minuscule bites, chewing thoroughly to make sure no bones went undetected and were swallowed.

"Don't eat it that way. I've told you before that you can't put anything else in your mouth with the fish. How are you going to find the bones if you do?" Mom handed me a piece of bread. "If a bone gets stuck in your throat, eat the bread to try to shake it loose when you swallow," she commanded.

It is a small wonder that a meal of fresh fish held no magic for me. On the contrary, it held the terror that I would die with a fish bone lodged in my throat.

Years later, when I was an older teen, I learned how to fillet fish. I learned that seldom does an errant fish bone get stuck in one's gullet, and even if it does, chances are that no harm will come of it. I also learned that if you have a mouthful of food and swallow, everything goes down with the flow.

Finally, I enjoyed the catch.

Chapter Forty-Six

"Get that thing out of here right this instant!" Mom screamed at me. "Don't put it over the pot of spaghetti! Eddie, I need your help, now!" Mom's voice was so shrill that Dad came barreling out of the outhouse with his pants hardly up.

By that time I was back outside, holding the arrow upon which I had impaled a ground squirrel. The poor thing was still alive and squirming around on the arrow. Dad quickly took it from me and hit it over the head with a piece of wood, killing it while Mom got on her hands and knees in the kitchen to wipe up gopher blood.

In those days, the thirteen lined ground squirrel, what we called the striped gopher, was considered a pest and a destructive critter by farmers although it did little harm unless it invaded a farmer's granary. I heard the opposite, however, from our neighbors and from Dad, and I went about ridding the county of the little burrowers with my bow. Dad thought I was doing a good turn for the farmers in whose fields I chased the furry things.

I was walking through the pines bordering our property one afternoon, and a red squirrel stuck its head around a tree. Its bright, beady eyes held me in its gaze, I raised my weapon, and I put an arrow right in the middle of the squirrel's chest.

"Dad, look at the shot I made!" I ran up to show him, elated. "It must have been ten yards away, and I hit it right in the chest."

What I didn't realize was that, in Dad's eyes, squirrels were in a different category than gophers. He enjoyed hearing them scolding from the trees. "You know, son, that was a good shot. You hit it right square. Now I want you to sit on your swing for a bit and think about what the squirrel ever did that you had to kill it."

I sat there a long time and couldn't come up with an answer. I never shot another thing in my life that I didn't have a use for nor did I use an animal for target practice again.

I did continue to hunt and trap ground squirrels, though, because in my mind, and Dad's, they were dastardly things that inflicted too much damage on the farmers' grain fields and pastures. I never took the time to test that idea to see if they actually were so destructive. I just went about the business of getting rid of them.

Sometime in my early years, I became fascinated with what might be inside of the animals I killed. I began to dissect them in a rudimentary fashion. I would skin them and look at the muscles. Then I would eviscerate them to find the organs inside. I was curious about their organs and what made them work.

This was not Mom's favorite of my pass-times. "Dennis, I told you to get that thing out of your room," Mom said, exasperated.

"It's starting to stink, and just look at the ants all over it. Don't bring any more dead animals into the house. Do you understand?"

"Mom, if you'd let me take that course on taxidermy that I read about in *Field and Stream*, I could do it so it wouldn't smell."

Until that time, I agreed to work in the shed.

Almost every week I'd try to stuff another specimen, usually a gopher or a dead bird I picked up along the road. I'd carefully skin one out and clean as much connective tissue from the hide as I could. I'd try to preserve everything with salt from Mom's cooking supplies. I never told her I was using the salt, and she never asked.

My biggest problem was always the head: I didn't know how to get the brains out. I would salt that down also, and then I'd pull the skin back over it. Then I called to Mom, "Do you have any cotton?"

"What do you need cotton for?" Mom asked suspiciously.

"I got this real nice gray gopher all skinned out and salted, but I need something to stuff it with."

"You are not going to waste any more cotton on those animals. Find some old rags and tear them up."

I stuffed the gopher with what I could find, sneaked a needle and thread, and then I sewed the hide up. Somehow, the gopher didn't look very alive, even when I tacked it to a piece of wood in an attempt to make it look like it was running along.

"What is that smell coming from your room, Dennis? You didn't drop a piece of lunch meat somewhere, did you?"

"No Mom, you told us we couldn't eat in there," I said innocently. When the coast was clear, I quietly reached under the bottom bunk bed and pulled out my latest attempt to preserve an animal. The small maggots around its mouth were repulsive enough to stop me from bringing my anatomical specimens into the house again.

Chapter Forty-Seven

One day when I was wandering on the forty acres next to our property, I sat down under an old branching pine. It was cool and peaceful in that spot. That's when I noticed a piece of bone sticking out of the fallen pine needles. I dug around a little, and just beneath the surface, I found a genuine bone yard.

Does that bone connect there? I wondered as I tried to piece them together. *Look at that, they fit, and they can bend back and forth at the joint. I wonder what kind of animal this was? Hey, there's the head over there. Look at the size of it! I bet this was a horse.*

I spent the rest of the day digging up bones and trying to match them to their partners.

"Dad, I found this neat skeleton in the woods today," I said over dinner. "It's in Al's woods. What do you think it is?"

"I remember a long time ago that Al had a big Percheron that was sick," Dad answered after a moment's thought. "I think he took it out there and shot it. I suppose that's what you've found."

"What's a Percheron?" I asked.

"It's a breed of work horse. We had them on the farm before the Depression. They were beautiful horses," Dad added.

I spent days working on that skeleton, and even after I had done all I could do, I returned to the spot to ponder my find.

This was my life. The nearest neighbor kid my age lived a mile away, and she was a girl. She didn't count as a playmate. My cousin Terry lived another two miles further away. His home was past the cow pasture with the bull, beyond the woods, and on the other side of the hayfield. Rarely did I make the journey to visit him.

I roamed the woods from morning to night, and I became a keen observer of plants and wildlife. I could sit for hours in one spot just to see what passed by. Some days I tried out new survival techniques.

"Come on Janice, try one." I held out something brown and crunchy to her. "They're good. Watch, I'm eating one."

Janice squirmed and ran away. "Mom, Dennis is trying to make me eat grasshopper legs," she tattled.

"Dennis, what are you doing out there? Stop pestering your sister. Your father will hear about this when he gets home."

I had sacrificed about fifty grasshoppers, removed their legs, and dropped them in my small mess-kit frying pan. I built a fire out of twigs and birch bark near my tent in the backyard, and I sautéed the delicacy.

With plenty of salt, they really didn't taste too bad. Janice missed out.

Chapter Forty-Eight

When I was only five, Uncle Bill gave me a dozen Victor number one animal traps. These were steel leg-hold traps designed to catch small animals. Dad showed me how to depress the spring and set the trigger and the tongue so I didn't catch my own fingers. He promised to teach me to trap in the fall.

"Dad, when am I going to be able to use my traps that Uncle Billy gave me?" I asked impatiently.

"I've told you before, we can't begin trapping until November," Dad answered, a little irked because I asked that question every day. "The animal pelts have to be prime or they're no good." We had to wait until the fur-bearers had their winter coats. In warmer weather, the furs were worthless as far as buyers were concerned.

"I think we'll set out your traps today, Dennis," Dad announced one Saturday morning in early November. "Get the stink bait from behind the garage and find the bag of duck feathers I had you put away a few weeks ago." When we were fishing during the summer, Dad had me keep some of the small perch we usually threw back. He told me to put them in a quart canning jar and seal the lid. Then we put them behind the garage. I checked every few days to see what was happening. The last time I looked, they had rotted to a gray, soupy mess in the jar.

We walked a few yards into the woods where Dad had piled some logs. "This looks like a good spot," Dad said, and he put the jar of bait on the ground. "Now set the trap like I showed you."

I depressed the spring with my foot and carefully set the jaws in the open position.

"Open the stink bait," he said. "Don't get any of it on your clothes, or your mother will skin both of us alive." I did as he instructed. Dad stirred the repulsive mixture with a small twig, and then he poured a tablespoon or so of the vile stuff on the ground under one of the overhanging logs. "Set your trap on top of where I poured the bait," he said. "Put a handful of feathers on the trap. Weasels sneak up on their prey and then pounce. He'll be attracted by the smell, and when he sees the feathers, he'll think it's a bird."

I did what Dad said, and we attached the chain of the trap to a stem of hazelnut brush. That way, if we caught an animal, it couldn't carry the trap away.

The next morning, I was up before anyone else. I dressed so fast I hardly buttoned my shirt before I rushed out to check my trap. I thought I saw a piece of white cotton on the bare ground, and I tried to figure out what might have fallen out of my pocket when we were setting the trap. When I got closer, though, I could see it was a weasel. Just as Dad had predicted, it dove into the feathers, and the trap had sprung and caught the weasel around the chest. The weasel was dead when I found it. I removed it from the trap and ran home with my prize.

"Dad, I caught one!" I shouted as I ran into Mom and Dad's bedroom.

"No kidding?" Dad said, sounding a little surprised. "Take it out on the porch. I'll be out in a second to look at it."

After Dad got up and dressed, he joined me outside. We admired the whiteness of the animal, and Dad commented about its black-tipped tail. "They have that little spot of black to help them blend in with their surroundings. It doesn't look like much to help them hide, but it must work," he stated. "We'd better get it skinned right away."

I watched intently as Dad, using his pocket knife, cut the skin between the weasel's back legs and then pulled the skin forward until it slipped off the weasel's head. The pelt was a tube, flesh side out. He had whittled a stretching board from a wooden slat he saved from a peach crate. Now he stretched the weasel skin over the board to dry.

"We let the skin dry for two weeks, and then you can sell it to the fur buyer," Dad said. "You can keep it in your room while it dries, if you want."

I sold the weasel pelt two weeks later and pocketed fifty cents.

Chapter Forty-Nine

For months, I planned my next trapping season. I planned to make a financial haul. But when the next November finally rolled around, my big plans got off to a slow start.

"I know you haven't had any luck around here with your trapping," Dad said sympathetically one evening. "Why don't we go to my stumpage this weekend and set a few traps? I've seen weasel tracks around some of my log piles."

That Saturday, we bundled up against the cold and headed out. Dad was right. Almost every pile had tracks where a weasel had probed the spaces between the logs. We set three traps.

Just my luck, I developed a high fever that night. Mom said there was no way I could go to check my traps.

"I'm going out to do some cutting this morning, Dennis," Dad told me sympathetically. "I'll be sure to check your traps for you."

He returned home in hardly enough time to drive to his stumpage and back. "Gen, do you know where the box of rifle shells is?" he asked excitedly.

Mom wondered why he needed his gun.

"I'll show you when I get back," he answered hurriedly, and he ran out the door with his rifle in hand. He returned an hour later and walked into my bedroom with a big smile on his face.

"Do you feel well enough to get up?" Dad asked. "I've got something outside you'll want to see." I scrambled out of bed and dressed in a hurry. Then I put on my winter jacket and followed Dad outside. "That's what was in your weasel trap when I got there." He pointed to what was laying on the ground. "It's a bobcat, the biggest I've ever seen."

I looked at it in shock. It was almost as long as I was tall.

"When I got there, I saw that something big had stepped in the trap, but it had broken the tether and pulled the trap away," Dad went on. "I could tell by the tracks it was a bobcat dragging the trap. It was easy to trail, and when I found it, I shot it."

I was still dumbfounded. All I could do was run my hands over the cat's coat. "There's a bounty on them, you know," Dad informed me. "All we have to do is take it to Bolsdorf, and he'll pay you."

Someone at the Grand Rapids newspaper, the *Herald Review*, heard about my catch. A reporter called my parents. I made the front page of the next edition, holding my frozen bobcat like a log.

I made three dollars that trapping season.

I was on my way to being rich. With my three dollars, I bought more traps. The next trapping season, when I was seven, Dad helped me set a trap line along the shore of Arvid's Lake. Three days later, I saw a telltale white ball next to my first trap. I had scored a weasel. The season had hardly started, and I was making money.

On Saturday, Dad asked, "Do you mind if I come with to look at your traps?" I agreed, and we stopped where the first trap was set. Nothing had disturbed the bird feather clump there. We moved 100 yards down the lake shore to the second trap. "You'll never catch anything here," Dad reprimanded. "You've moved your trap right out in the open." He pulled up the trap. Using a stick, he dug a hole under an exposed tree root. Then he put the trap in the six inch hole and baited it. I was getting angry by then that he was taking over.

We walked on. From a distance, I could see that the ground was torn up around the next trap. "What do you think I caught?" I asked Dad, immediately thinking bobcat.

"I can't tell," Dad said. "You stay here until I find out what it is." I stood as he crept up to the spot."Come see," he called eventually.

When I came to where he was standing, I saw a cylinder of black fur stretched out on the ground. It shimmered in the late afternoon sunlight. "What is it?" I asked.

"It's a mink," Dad informed me. "They're worth a lot of money right now. About thirty dollars for this one, I'd guess."

Thirty dollars! Dad let me keep the money when we sold the pelt, and I bought more traps, more arrows, and more BBs for my gun. Then I began calculating in earnest. Ten mink times thirty dollars. That's three hundred dollars! Over the next week, I spent those three hundred dollars twenty different ways.

On Friday night, Mom had invited company for dinner. She was taking the potatoes off the stove and getting ready to mash them when I said I was going to run and check my traps. I was sure I'd have another mink by this time.

"You can go," she said, a little irritated with me. "But Max and Pearl will be here soon. I don't want you late."

I ran to the lake and up to where my first trap was set. Nothing. Breathlessly, I approached my second set, the one Dad had placed in the hole in the sandy bank. I could see that something was in the trap, but it had burrowed deep under the tree root. I got down on my hands and knees and peered into the hole. I could see shiny, black fur that looked like mink. This time, the animal was still alive. I tried to pull it from the hole, but it wouldn't budge. I raced home.

"Dad!" I shouted. "I've got another one, but I can't get it out from under the tree root."

Dad jumped up and put on his jacket. "If Max and Pearl get here before we come back, tell them we won't be long," Dad said over his shoulder to Mom as we went out the door.

It took only a few minutes to reach my catch. Dad looked in the hole. "It sure looks like mink fur," Dad said as he peered into the dark hole at the little bit of fur he could see. He started peeling away the duff that covered the hole. "Get back!" he yelled as a black and white striped head popped up. But it was too late. Fortunately, the skunk didn't hit either one of us directly. Using a long pole Dad was able to depress the trap spring enough that the skunk pulled its leg free so it could wobble away into the brush.

Dad said not to rush getting home. He thought fresh air might help. When we entered the kitchen, our company had arrived.

"Where is it?" Mom asked expectantly, looking for our mink. She wrinkled her nose. "Oh." That was all she said.

Chapter Fifty

Once I was watching Dad and our neighbor, Al, as they hauled logs from the water of Arvid's Lake. Mom came running down the bank on the other side of the lake. When she yelled to us, I couldn't hear.

"What's she saying?" Dad asked. "Can you hear her, Al?"

"No, I can't make it out."

"WE CAN'T HEAR YOU," Dad shouted back. "WHAT DID YOU SAY?"

This time Mom yelled louder and slower. "THE DAM BROKE AGAIN! KATHRYN JUST CALLED."

"I think she said the dam broke again," Dad told to Al excitedly. "Let's get to the mouth of the creek."

Several days earlier, the dam in Grand Rapids that held back the Mississippi River had broken, sending a torrent of water rushing downstream. The riverbed was able to absorb most of the runoff, and no damage had been done to homes or property.

That dam had two purposes in Grand Rapids, however: it formed a reservoir of water for the Blandin Paper Mill, and it served as a place where the mill rafted its logs before they were processed. With the release of water, tens of thousands of pulpwood logs cascaded down the river.

Many of the logs had gotten jammed near the creek coming out of Arvid's Lake, and the lake was literally filled with wood. Dad and Al had strung a five-eighths inch steel cable across the lake and devised a pulley system to snake the wayward pulp sticks to shore.

They had salvage rights. The lake had been almost cleared of logs when the dam broke again.

"I'm sticking a twig at the water's edge, Dennis," Dad said. "I want you to watch it and tell us if the water is rising or falling."

"Here they come, Ed." Al was staring upstream. "Holy cow, look at that! They must have put a whole new batch of logs in the pond before it broke again."

"Dad, the water's still rising!" I called to him. "It's up about two inches, and it's still going up."

Dad gestured to Al. "Come on! There's more coming down. I think we can salvage even more this time."

It was an absolutely frantic time with the men trying to create a log jam so more logs would push into Arvid's Lake, me trying to keep track of the water level, and the river gaining more force with each passing minute. "The river's starting to drop, Dad! It's almost down to where it started."

"Yeah, the logs have quit coming down, too. I think we filled the lake from bank to bank. They're even backed up to the creek."

"We might as well get busy dragging them out, Ed," Al said, beaming. "There must be a couple hundred cords! It'll take us the better part of the week to snake them out."

I remember Dad joking that he recognized logs that he'd cut and sold to the mill. "Yup, that's one of mine," he laughed

By the end of the week, Dad and our neighbor had a huge stack of pulpwood piled up on our land, and it was time to negotiate with the paper mill to see what they would pay to get their wood back.

Chapter Fifty-One

"Mom, look at this bike in the catalogue. Isn't it a beauty?"

"Which one are you looking at?" Mom peered over my shoulder at the catalogue.

"The black one with white trim," I answered wistfully. "It has a built in horn and a headlight. When do you think I can get a bike?"

"Probably not this summer," Mom said regretfully. "It sounds like Dad will be on strike, and we might be short for a while."

With that, I quit asking about a bike, but I never quit dreaming. Every chance I got, I sat with the catalogue admiring that black bike. I pictured myself riding to my cousins' or pedaling to the store to pick up groceries.

The miners did go on strike that summer. Week after week, Dad picked up whatever employment he could find. He cleared brush from the ditches for the township, work that paid less than a dollar an hour. True to his nature, Dad toiled as hard for that wage as he would have for much more. Other times, he worked for farmers or picked up odd jobs.

One night, he and Max, the owner of the Blackberry Store, went for a ride in Max's car. Later, Max stopped by our house, and over coffee, they joked and laughed about running across a potato field and hitting a barbed wire fence. They especially howled when Max kidded Dad about tripping and losing his shotgun in the dark. Apparently Dad had to grope around in the brush until he found his gun. I was confused. I pictured Dad cart-wheeling through the air, but I didn't know what he was doing in a field with his shotgun in the dead of night.

I figured it out the next night when we had fresh meat for supper. Mom said it was beef, but it sure tasted like the venison that Dad brought home in the fall during deer season. It wasn't deer season now.

We did what we had to in order to survive.

"Come on, Dennis," Dad said to me one afternoon. "Get Janice. We're going into town."

"Do I have to go?" I complained. "I want to build a lean-to, and we just went to town a couple of days ago."

"Come on," Dad cajoled. "This is important."

Dad had put the top carriers on the car, so evidently we were getting something pretty large. He drove to Grand Rapids and right up to the Montgomery Wards catalogue store.

"What's in that box, Dad?" I asked after he had tied it on the top carriers. "It looks heavy."

"Wait until we get home," he said. "Then you can help me unpack it." When it was unloaded at the house, Dad took his pocket knife, and he cut the box apart.

Inside were the pieces to a shiny black and white bicycle. To this day, I don't know how they came up with the money, but Mom and Dad had bought me the bike I had dreamed about.

Dad assembled it with little problem, and I went wobbling off down the road. Since I'd learned how to ride my cousin's bike, I was soon going full speed down the country road.

Then Mom tried it, and she, too, was able to ride.

"Come on, Eddie, give it a try," she called to Dad.

Dad shook his head. "Naw, I don't think so."

Mom coaxed until eventually Dad got on and tried to peddle. The bike began to topple sideways, and he had to put his foot down to catch himself. He tried again.

"Mom, can't Dad ride a bicycle?" I asked quietly.

"Your dad never had a bicycle. I think this is the first time he's been on one."

I knew my parents had made a sacrifice for me. I went to bed that night happy I had my bike, but somehow, I felt like I had gotten something I shouldn't have.

Chapter Fifty-Two

Dad and I were at a lumberyard in Grand Rapids. It was a relatively new yard, and the owner was a newcomer to the area. He recognized only a few of the locals by name.

Dad picked out some lumber and was standing at the counter, ready to pay. "Doggone it! I forgot my wallet at home." He shook his head in disbelief as he dug in his pockets. "I never do that. You don't suppose I could take the lumber home and pay you tomorrow when I come back for another load?" he asked the owner.

"Sorry, we don't extend credit," the man behind the counter said. "It has to be cash now. You will have to unload what you've picked out. That's our policy."

There was another man by the counter. "Just a minute, Ray," the man said. "I'll vouch for him. This is Ed Herschbach, and if he says he'll be back with your money tomorrow, he will."

We drove away with the load of lumber, but I took home something else. That day I was proud to be Dad's son, and I'll never forget the look in Dad's eyes when the man spoke up for him.

I was always tagging along with either Mom or Dad. I was comfortable being in the woods with Dad, and when Mom took me into the blueberry patches in the forest, I was at home. But when we went to Grand Rapids, I never did get used to the people and the speed of traffic. I was amazed at the sight of three story buildings.

One thing I did enjoy was riding on the Greyhound Bus to town. Mom, Janice, and I would walk to the Blackberry Store, and we would flag down the Greyhound Bus coming from Duluth to

Grand Rapids. Mom could shop all day if we took the bus, and Dad would meet us at a prearranged spot when he finished work.

I browsed in the sporting goods stores, and I sometimes bought a new arrow with my potato bug money to replace one I had lost. I never went far from Mom. Grand Rapids was just too big for me. Eventually, I would go with Mom into Kamen's, a women's apparel shop. As soon as we got into the store, I'd look out for the sales lady.

She was absolutely gorgeous, knock-down, drag-out gorgeous. Her long, dark hair was pulled back from her face, and not one single strand was awry. It was held there by a set of fancy, sparkling combs. Her mouth was outlined in bright red lipstick, and she shaped her eyebrows in just the right arch to draw attention to her deep brown eyes.

Her legs were as perfect as the rest of her. Long and slender, they were accentuated by three-inch spike heels. She *must* have been beautiful, because when I saw her for the first time, my jaw dropped to the floor—and I was only six years old. I was absolutely in awe of that beautiful lady/salesperson/model. She even had an exotic name. Yvonne was a sight to behold: gorgeous, sophisticated, and dressed to the hilt.

Mom was a country housewife, and she had two or three "go to town" dresses that were always a little faded. She was about six years younger than Yvonne and hardly came to Yvonne's shoulder. My mother was nice looking, evenly proportioned, and intelligent, but her reservoir of self-esteem was only about half as big as she was tall.

Mom shriveled inwardly when Yvonne approached her with a confident smile. They always spoke civilly to each other, but I knew that Mom felt like crawling on the sidewalk after we left the store. She went there only to dream; she couldn't afford to buy. I knew she wanted to have clothes like Yvonne, and I knew she wished she was tall and sophisticated. I knew she thought having to trek to the outhouse in the rain was demeaning. That must have been why Mom seemed especially small to me when she was around Yvonne.

Later, I learned a little bit of Dad's past. It seems that before Dad met Mom, he and Yvonne had been an item. They had known each other for years, and to many, it appeared they were on the way to marriage. Something happened, however, to break it off.

In my naïve thinking, I couldn't understand why Mom was so intimidated. After all, she was the one Dad had married. She was the one with whom he had parented children. She was the one to whom he was faithful. It seemed to me she had won.

Years later, after Dad's funeral, I mentioned Yvonne while Janice and I were talking about Mom and Dad.

"You know what really happened there, don't you?" Janice asked.

"Dad had dated Yvonne before he met Mom, right?" I half asked, half stated. "That's why Mom always felt so uncomfortable around her."

"I guess you *don't* know." Janice volunteered to fill me in.

One Saturday night before Mom and Dad got together, Dad and Yvonne had gone on a date. It was a double date, and Dad's buddy, Jerry, had a new car that was built for speed. It had a flathead six for a motor, and it could *go*. Dad and Yvonne were in the backseat when Dad's buddy lost control, and the car flipped as it left the roadway. Yvonne was thrown out of the vehicle, and it rolled over her, crushing her pelvis and inflicting a multitude of traumatic injuries to her body. Miraculously, she lived, and she was rushed to the hospital where she convalesced for weeks. She recovered fully, but her hospital bills were staggering.

After the accident, Dad shouldered all of the responsibility for Yvonne's hospital bills. He reasoned that if he hadn't asked her to go out that night and allowed his friend to drive, the accident wouldn't have happened. Janice didn't say it, but I suspect that alcohol was probably involved.

Dad paid off the entire medical bill for Yvonne. Because of the size of the debt, he was still paying on it when he met Mom. He continued to send money after he married Mom, even though he and Mom didn't have the proverbial pot to pee in.

Finally, I knew the cause of the tension between Mom and Yvonne. I can only imagine that Mom must have wondered if Dad still had a "thing" for that tall brunette with the fancy clothes, and it dawned on me that Yvonne was able to buy those fancy clothes because she wasn't in debt. On the other hand, Mom couldn't afford one new dress.

Yvonne's injuries must have healed well. I think she had at least one child, but more importantly, my parent's marriage must have healed, too. They were married fifty-four years.

Chapter Fifty-Three

My brother, Bill, was born in early August of 1953, and our crowded house became even more cramped. Janice and I still shared a bedroom with bunk beds even though I was well past ten and my sister was old enough to be in school. Our parents planned to add two bedrooms to the house.

"I was thinking," Mom said, "that if we divided what is now the kids' bedroom, we could make a room big enough for Bill and still have room for a small bathroom. What do you think, Eddie?"

"If we did that, we'd need to dig a new well. Then what about our septic system? If we put more water into the one we have, it will fail. We can't afford a new septic tank and drain field."

Our system was not much of a system as it was. Dad had dug a very large hole, filled it with head-sized stones, covered it with tarpaper, and then shoveled dirt on top. This was our dry well, the place where dishwater and wash water could drain into and then percolate into the soil. It would never handle the waste from a flush toilet or the volume of water from a shower or bathtub.

Mom wouldn't give up. "We can borrow money for a well and septic system. We don't owe anyone, and we certainly qualify for a loan."

By this time Dad was getting tired of the repeated argument about a bathroom. "We'll think about it."

Dad had dug the basement using a scraper and a team of horses. Now, he dug the trenches for the foundation of the new addition by hand with a long handled shovel. The addition had two bedrooms, one for me and the other for Janice, but there was no place for a bathroom. Dad started the project during the summer before Bill's birth, and by the time he and Mom came home from the hospital, the walls were up. It was time to put a roof over the old and the new.

"How are you going to do this, Eddie?" Mom wanted to know. I could tell by the look on her face that she really didn't trust him to get the job done right.

"I've got Hub and Wilfred coming tomorrow, and their boys will be with. Glenn said he'd be here, too, and I think Don is coming over. We'll have a good crew. If we start early, we'll have the old roof off by noon and the new one on by supper." Dad sounded confident, but I could tell he wasn't as sure as he wanted to be.

The next day the crew showed up, and they tackled the old roof. It was four sided, four triangles that met in a peak at the center of the house, and it came down quickly, more quickly than Dad had predicted.

My brother was only two weeks old and sleeping soundly in his crib. Everyone laughed at how he could sleep through all of the pounding and ripping noises going on over his bed.

Suddenly, I heard a crash, and Mom shrieked, "My baby!"

I rushed into their bedroom and found Mom holding my brother. Bill was covered with dusty insulation, and a two-by-four lay across his bed, propping up a large piece of ceiling. Dad was looking down through the hole in the ceiling with an anguished expression. "Is he okay, Gen? Is he breathing? Is there any blood?" Dad was scared.

One of the two-by-four ceiling joists had rotted, and when Dad stepped on it, it broke in two and crashed down on Bill's crib. Fortunately, the piece was long enough that it bridged across the crib. Otherwise my brother would most certainly have been crushed as he slept.

All Mom could do was glare at Dad. Whenever mishaps occurred, it was always seemed to be his fault, and this threat to her child was not taken well. She cradled my brother in her arms while she wept and verbally attacked at the same time, her frustrations boiling over like a pressure cooker blowing its relief valve.

Mom hated the way things were always done on the cheap. She hated the mess, and she hated the fact that things never turned out the way she dreamed. She hated the country and not having a bathroom. At that point, she hated her life.

Chapter Fifty-Four

By the time winter set in, the new addition was completely enclosed and windows were installed. Still, there was no door from the living room into either of the newly added rooms. When we went into the addition (I was expected to work out there in the unheated area with Dad), we crawled through the living room window. Mom could tell that her vision for the new living space was not going to be what the finished product resembled. All she could see was the mess that was being created every day.

For my part, I could hardly wait to have my own room. I could see my BB gun hanging from a set of deer antlers on the wall. I would stand my bow and arrows in the corner by the window.

What Mom saw was something quite different. She saw a floor made of the cheapest wood, a floor that would be impossible to clean. She saw threadbare bedspreads and unfinished baseboards. She saw a lifetime of using an outhouse, a lifetime of raising and canning vegetables, a lifetime of berry picking.

Dad saw something taking shape that was far better than what he had when he grew up. He saw a functional house that kept out the rain and the snow and a home he had worked hard to provide.

That winter, the progress slowed to a crawl and then stopped completely, but I was too busy to notice or care. Winter adventures were different from my summer escapades: no mosquitoes, no deer flies or horseflies, and no poison ivy. For me, the cold was easier to tolerate than the heat. Decked out in my choppers, wool socks, a cap with ear flaps, and my winter coat, I was warm enough to roam the forest on even the coldest days.

Once, I was trudging through new fallen snow, and I spotted a place where the snow was pockmarked as if a struggle had gone on. I could make out the dark outline of the animal's body lying under the surface. I figured that a rabbit had been attacked by a predator, had died, and had been left for some reason by the attacker. I carefully approached, reading the signs of what had happened in the snow. Then I reached down to retrieve the fallen cottontail.

When I touched it, it exploded in my face. I was blinded with flying snow, surprised that the thing had come to life, and I was shocked by a whirring, drumming noise so close to my ears. My legs gave out from under me, and I sat down with a whoomp! into a foot-and-a-half of snow. My heart was beating so fast that I thought I was dying, and I had trouble breathing.

After a few seconds, it dawned on me what had happened. Ruffed grouse bury themselves in the snow as protection from the cold winter air. I had stumbled on one that hadn't done too good a job of hiding and was evidently a sound sleeper. Its heart was probably beating faster than mine.

And so the winter passed. I was comfortable at school, and I had developed some close friendships. I had actually fallen in love with the girl who sat behind me in class, in love as only a fifth grade boy can be. Each day the sun traveled higher in the sky, and the unmistakable smell of spring was in the March breeze. I knew it wouldn't be long before I would have time to live like I wanted to live, carefree in the woods.

That summer I was going to be eleven years old, and Dad had promised me that when I was eleven, I could go down to the lake and fish by myself. I'd seen our neighbor, Bill Van Quackelberg, fishing near the drop off in the lake when Mom and I had walked down together. He had a stringer of crappies, a couple of bullheads, and even a northern pike. I could hardly wait for my turn.

Not only that, but the fall before, I had made a discovery that fueled my fishing ambitions. While digging a hole in the woods, I uncovered earthworms. I'd never found worms in the sandy jack pine soil around our house, and these were real worms, not skinny little threads. They were the fat, juicy kind that any fish would jump out of the water to grab.

I saw life as being one continuous outdoor adventure. How could anyone not love this place? This was my home, all I had ever known, and I had no thought of ever leaving.

Chapter Fifty-Five

As a child, life was full of questions for me. At the time, I couldn't figure out why Mom hated the country so; I knew no other way of life. I couldn't figure out why she always walked as though she were in a panicked hurry, or why she acted so insecure when we were in town. I didn't know why Dad treated me well and then turned around and said cruel things to me an instant later.

"Why in the hell don't you pick up your feet when you walk You're tripping all the time."

It didn't matter that I had fallen down and skinned my knee or that I was crying. I was thirty years old before I began to figure Dad out. When I fell and was injured, he had two choices: cry with me or get angry. If he was angry he didn't cry. Men didn't cry.

There were a number of questions that I harbored but never asked my parents. Still, I recognized that there was always tension present in our home.

Sometime during the winter of 1953-54, my parents made a decision of which I was unaware. I can imagine the conversations that went on after my sister and I were in bed.

"Eddie, I can't stand this life anymore. Maybe it would be better if we divorced. You could stay here, and I'd go back to Keewatin. Something has to change."

I imagine Dad rolling his eyes upward as he so often did and answering, "What do you expect of me? No matter what I do, it isn't good enough for you. I'm a miner, that's what I do. Can't you get it through your head?"

I heard enough arguments to know what Mom would have said. "Look at you. Every day you come home from work covered with ore. It's in your clothes, in your hair, in your skin. Everything I wash is stained red from what you bring home. Doesn't it bother you to live this way?"

"I think I've given you a pretty good life," Dad would answer. "At least you've never been hungry or without heat."

"But Eddie, we could live so differently! Look at this ad in last Sunday's paper. There's a small Red Owl grocery store for sale in Pine River. We could work it together. I worked at the Blackberry Store before we were married. I could certainly work the till, and you're good with numbers. Between the two of us, we could make a good team."

Dad was always fearful of taking a risk.

"Gen, I'd have to quit the mine, and I'd lose my eight years of seniority. I started at the Danube Mine in '37, and if I hadn't quit and then gone back in '44, I'd have fourteen years with the company by now. I'd even be ahead of Vic on the seniority list. I think it's a bad idea for me to quit again."

But Mom would have done her research. "You can take a six-month leave of absence and not lose a day on the list."

When Mom sunk her teeth into something, she wouldn't give it up. Without my knowledge, they decided to borrow some money from Grandpa Burns. By selling our house, they would have enough money to buy the store and move us to Pine River.

I can't remember anyone telling me about this decision, discussing it with my sister and me, or even preparing us for the move. Late one afternoon near the end of May, Mom told us we should all get cleaned up, that we were going to the town hall. I wondered what was going on. The only time we went there was for the annual Christmas program or some other special occasion. When we arrived, most of Blackberry was already there.

I was confused and felt extremely out of place. Men were shaking Dad's hand, and women were hugging Mom. A couple of folding tables were covered with food, and I could smell coffee brewing. Someone asked me if I had seen the new place we were moving to. That is how I discovered we were leaving.

I remember a shoe box decorated with a cutout of the Red Owl logo sitting on a coffee table, and as people passed, they dropped money into the slot cut in the top. Then the program started. Men began to tell about how hard Dad worked, how honest he was, and what a great woodsman he was.

A man named Erickson stood up. "I remember Ed looking at some timber on my property that I wanted logged off. We left my place one evening to get an idea of what I had, and before we could get out of the woods, it started to get dark. I wouldn't have known which way to go, but Ed went through the brush like it was daylight. I'd go anywhere in the woods with that guy and not be afraid of getting lost."

The evening went on until everything was said that was going to be said. We ate the potluck meal and then headed home.

"Dad and I didn't tell you we were moving. We didn't want to worry you," Mom said when I asked what was going on. "In a week we'll pack up everything and drive to our new home. I think you'll like it. We'll live in town where you can walk to the movie theater. You'll be able to play baseball every day. Because we're moving in early summer, you'll have time to make friends before school starts."

I blocked the next week out of my mind. I have no recollection of the time before we moved.

Chapter Fifty-Six

Dad pulled into our driveway with a battered, red-faded-to-orange flatbed truck, and he parked it on the lawn by the front door.

"Eddie, be careful with that headboard!" Mom pleaded, her forehead wrinkled with lines of exertion and exasperation. "It's the only decent piece of furniture we have."

Dad, straining to keep the heavy object upright, shot back, "Lift your end a little higher, then. I can't do this alone."

"Look what you did now!" Mom almost wailed. "You scraped its face across the door latch. It dug right through the finish. Now we have another piece of junk."

Dad wasn't concerned. "Just put on an extra heavy coat of wax. No one will notice."

Boxes and bags were piled onto the truck and tied down with hay ropes and clothesline. By this time, a couple of neighbors had stopped by to help, and our old sofa and chair were lifted onto the truck bed. When the loading was done, it looked like the Beverly Hillbillies were leaving town.

Mom wondered what was going to happen if it started to rain, and Dad said it wasn't going to. He was always so sure he was right, but the trip was over sixty miles. Just because the sun was shining in Blackberry didn't mean it was shining in Pine River. Fortunately, Dad really was right this time.

Mom, my sister, my brother, and myself rode in a car with a friend of Dad's. Mom wasn't too thrilled about that arrangement, and she complained to Dad that she didn't like the idea of riding sixty miles with an unmarried man who was a stranger. Dad just said there wasn't room in the truck for all of us, and that was the way it was going to be. He drove the truck, and we followed, stopping eventually in front of a two story house that had a flush toilet, a house that we would call home for four months.

Chapter Fifty-Seven

We unpacked, put the boxes in the right rooms, placed the furniture near the spots Mom said, and stocked the cupboards. Then Dad said he needed to return the truck to his friend in Blackberry. I went with him, and as usual, we rode without talking most of the way. Dad didn't look too happy, that I remember.

Dad delivered the truck to its owner. Back in the car, he turned to me. "I have to meet with Mr. Wilson, the man who bought our house, to finish a few details of the sale. We're going to stop by the old place for a few minutes."

I rode in silence to what had been home. I didn't want to see Mr. Wilson because, in my mind, he was the one who had taken away so much of what I loved.

While Dad talked to Mr. Wilson, I aimlessly walked over to the clump of birches where my tent had been perennially pitched. I ran my fingers over their white bark, pressed my cheek against their smoothness, and smelled the freshness of early-summer leaves.

I sat on my swing. When I was eight, Dad had made it by cutting a rubber tire to form two rings and a seat. As I swung, I looked south at a future forest, then only saplings hardly older than I was. My throat tightened, and I swung harder, kicking at the dry jack pine sand that passed beneath my feet. Then I let the swing pendulum to a stop and sat still, listening to the wind rustle the leaves of the quaking aspens.

Dad finished his business and walked over to me. I noticed him swallow hard, as if he had something in his throat that wouldn't go down, and he stared out over what had been his potato patch and garden. He ran his fingers over the swing rope and picked at the bark of one of the pines that supported the swing.

I imagine he was thinking of digging the basement, of the sweat and aching muscles. Perhaps he was remembering the time the axe split his big toe or of the piles of firewood he had stacked on the back porch.

"Are you okay?" he asked me after several minutes.

With my head turned away from him, I nodded. I didn't want him to see the tears that ran down my cheeks. I got off the swing, walked to the car, and rode home looking out the side window. I stared as the trees sped by, as we passed the spot where I had seen the mother grouse with her chicks and the corner where the Blackberry School had stood, but I never looked back. I couldn't. My throat ached from stifling sobs.

After we moved from Blackberry, we lived in so many places I can't remember them all, and I was forced to attend so many different schools that they blend together. Following our brief stay in Pine River, we always lived in or near Grand Rapids and Coleraine, moving from house to house, sometimes within the boundaries of one school, sometimes another. During that time, Dad went back to work in the mines until, fifteen years later, he was granted his disability claim. I have no clue as to why my parents couldn't settle, but memories from my preteen and teen years almost don't exist.

I attended Grand Rapids Junior High School. In seventh grade, the Warba boys' basketball team came to Grand Rapids to play a game. As I watched from the stands, Jimmy, Rodney, and the others from Warba passed the ball around. I could hardly choke back my tears. After the game, I hurried down to the floor to say hi. They were talking and laughing with each other, and when I approached them, Jimmy turned to me and said, "How's it going?"

Just then, their coach shouted, "Okay, get those balls in the bag. We have to get back to Warba." A couple of the guys waved as they went out the door, and then they were gone. With a stab of remorse I realized I no longer belonged with them.

Dad struggled to find his identity as well. Living in town was difficult for him, and he was never content with neighbors so close on either side. He missed cutting wood. He missed his garden.

"Come on, Dennis," he called to me one day. "I want to drive out to Little Cow Horn." Little Cow Horn was a lake Dad had hunted at the opener of duck season for most of his life. Now, three weeks before duck season, he said he wanted to go there to see if anything was flying.

That September day, as we walked down the leaf-strewn logging road to the lake, he confided in me, something he hardly ever did.

"I don't know what it is. I can't seem to get excited about hunting anymore. I might not even hunt ducks this fall." I listened, but I couldn't think of anything to say to him. "With Don dying of lung cancer, it wouldn't be the same," he continued. Don had been his duck hunting companion as well as his logging partner. "Anyway, I don't think I want to kill anything anymore," he said. "I've done enough of that in my life."

We walked down to the lake in silence and watched the distant ducks swarm like bees over the lake. Then we returned to the car.

While I buried my thoughts in books, Dad had few outlets for his interests. Our outings became less frequent, and for a few years, hardly ever happened. Once in a while he would take in a baseball game or a high school track meet, but mostly he worked in the mine, fished a little, and watched the first television we owned.

I read volumes of books about teenage boys having exciting adventures in the woods or on deserted South Pacific islands. More and more I fell into a world of dreams and wishes.

Mom took a job in a greenhouse and flower shop. She seemed to bloom along with the flowers, and she told me she wished she could buy the place and have it for her own. I think she was happier there than anyplace she worked.

Janice and Bill were still too young to realize what was going on, although I think it was harder on Janice than we realized. She, like me, attended a number of schools while Mom and Dad moved from place to place.

Only two weeks before he died somewhat unexpectedly of a heart attack, I visited Dad at his assisted living home in Grand Rapids. He was eighty-six years old. His hands and forearms were still massive, but his body was bent and twisted. Because of the injury he had sustained in the mine, his back had deteriorated into a contorted mess of bone spurs and calcium deposits scattered on either side of his spine. X-ray technicians marveled at the fact that he could even walk.

Though Mom had died three years earlier, his blue eyes still held a sparkle, and his pure white hair was neatly combed to one side. He told me about showing his housekeeper his track medals, and how she said he must have been a great athlete. He laughed when he said that.

Then, from out of nowhere he said to me, "I wasn't a very good father to you when you were growing up."

"That's not true at all," I tried to assure him.

"Yes, it is," Dad continued, fidgeting with the buttons on his cardigan sweater. "It hurt you bad when we moved from Blackberry. I am so sorry I did that to you."

We sat in silence a few long seconds before I could speak.

"Dad, you did the best you could. I couldn't have asked for more."

In recent years, I have felt the need to drive through Blackberry, but every road is paved with asphalt. The logging trail on what was Dave Anderson's property (where Dad and I flushed eleven grouse one evening) has been converted to a dead end street between four houses.

I can hardly recognize any of the old landmarks. A stand of mature aspen trees is visible from the county road. They are the same trees that were the saplings I stared at while I sat on my swing for the last time. When I see them, I am home again, just for an instant. Home again to a place where the yellow sand is thin and fine, to a time when we made our own syrup from brown sugar stored in the tin in our cupboard.

Dennis Herschbach

Dennis Herschbach is a retired biology teacher who started writing as therapy following the death of his wife. His first book, *Grief Journey*, was published in 2007. Since then he has moved on from writing about grief and is active in the writing community of Duluth, Minnesota. In 2009, he took first place in the annual *Talking Stick* writing competition through the Jack Pine Writers Bloc for his short story "Filling a Hole." He is currently secretary of the League of Minnesota Poets and serves on the board of directors of the Lake Superior Writers.

Publisher Acknowledgements

Red Step Press would like to extend thanks to the following:

Kelly O'Brien, for taking the cover photo and learning how to use Photoshop in order to design the cover;

John Muckala, for his thoughtful editing of the book;

Becky O'Brien and Kelly O'Brien, for copyediting the book at the last minute when several readers backed out;

Hilarie Sorenson, Leah Kirchoff, and Jesse Bailey for their help copyediting;

Sarah Stonich, for her time and kind words;

Elizabeth Cleveland at Friesens, for her help and patience;

David O'Brien, for providing Red Step Press with our "state of the art" storage facility;

And Dennis Herschbach, for his diligent work on this manuscript and his persistence that, yes, this was the next book that Red Step Press wanted to publish!